Praise for *Runways*

"I finished your book last night and I just wanted to say thank you. What an incredible call you have on your life and I am thankful for the many things I have learned from reading this incredible book! Your tuned-in ear to the Holy Spirit has inspired a whole new level in me. THANK YOU!"

Isaiah Hollis
Executive Pastor
The Power Place Church, Pennsylvania

"I read most of the book in one night and finished it the next morning. I couldn't put it down. It was so inspiring and such a blessing! I want six more for Christmas gifts."

Jim Kirkland
Athens, Texas

"This is a book about what God can do when you allow the Holy Spirit to guide and direct your life. What an impact for the cause of Christ this man has made! It inspires one to listen more closely to the Holy Spirit and do what he is prompting.

Jane Ohlrogge
Denver, Colorado

"I read the book cover-to-cover in one night. It is so good!"

Reneta Steighaus
Arvada, Colorado

"There is a great anointing on *Runways* and now I want more of the Holy Spirit."

Anonymous

"I read the book in half a day, then packaged it up and sent it to my wife in Greece."

Shea Rouser, Texas

"I loved the book! It was so inspiring and I couldn't put it down. I sent it to my sister in Texas."

Rose Zorens,
Lakewood, Colorado

"Worth your time…a wonderful and well-written book about how a very ordinary man has done extraordinary things for God by stepping out in faith. It gave me real hope in the power and presence of God in our lives.

Mary K. Reed
Denver, Colorado

"*Runways of the Heart* has encouraged my faith greatly and I have some new runways to open in my life."

Diane Brask
Global Seed Planters
Shell Lake Wisconsin

"We have been so excited about the book, *Runways of the Heart*. We have given away three copies and each one of the recipients has had the same reaction. Our home group leaders said they want to meet the man who wrote this book. Georgia said she couldn't put the book down. This book is an inspiration that the Holy Spirit is alive and still guides our steps if we engage Him. [We are] re-energized to call on the Holy Spirit at all times."

Eldon and Elma Becker
Arizona

"October 2018 my heart was being drawn to serving in missions, but I wasn't sure what my next steps should be. My brother-in-law suggested I read *Runways of the Heart*. Shortly after that, I coincidentally ran into Pastor Russ at my church, Faith Bible Chapel. He gave me a copy of the book and I read it from cover-to-cover in two days. Pastor Russ's journey and the stories told were conveyed in such a way that it struck me, 'I can do this too!' And... the idea of starting a Bible Training Center bore witness in my spirit and propelled me to find out more.

"Because of what I read in the book, I met with Pastor Jason Holland [Executive Vice President for Joshua Nations] and attended a two-day training session. I am now studying the Joshua Nations curriculum at the new Faith Bible Chapel - Bible U that Pastor Russ helped start. I wait with great anticipation for whatever the Lord wants to do."

Shelley L. Rodriguez
Westminster, Colorado

"I couldn't put it down."

Patsy Hyman
Houston, Texas

"I was reading *Runways of the Heart* on my flight home from Phoenix to Denver. I noticed the lady next to me was reading the same book! I asked her where she got hers.

"'My pastor suggested it,' she said

"'Who is your pastor?' I asked.

"'Scott Applegate of Novation church in Westminster.'

"'I know him, and have worked with him, too!' I said. What a divine coincidence!

"I've known Pastor Russ for years, but didn't know all his escapades until I read this book! He is so candid and honest, from drinking to how he met Lana to the journey with Joshua Nations. I liked the sidebar stories and the stories in Part Two as well. My Bible study group went through his workbook on the Holy Spirit and they loved it! He lets the Holy Spirit lead him wherever he goes."

Judy Galasso
Arvada, Colorado

"I want eight more books for my grandkids for Christmas."

Sandy Albus
Pennsylvania

Runways of the Heart

My Journey Empowered by the Holy Spirit

From College Drunk to Founder of Joshua Nations, Initiating 7,300 Bible Training Centers in More than 60 Countries

By Dr. Russ Frase, Jr.

with Marla Lindstrom Benroth

Celebrating 50 Years of Ministry

I dedicate this book to Lana, my loving wife of 50 years, who has given me up to the Lord's service. Her love, patience, and understanding have made 50 years (so far) of ministry possible.

I also dedicate this book to our children, Paula Romer and Rusty Frase, who allowed their Daddy to be gone far more than he should have. The understanding and steadfast love of my family created much space for others in my life.

Table of Contents

Foreword

Every real born-again believer wants to discover God's will for their lives, but so few realize their God-given purpose or experience the power Jesus promised with the coming of the Holy Spirit. In this book you will read about someone who has done both. Through Pastor Russ's life story you can discover key principles that guided and empowered his life and thus equip your own life as well.

I have known Pastor Russ for more than 30 years now and have seen him walk a Spirit-filled life like few I have ever met. His ability to love God with all his heart and his willingness to sacrifice for the sake of sharing the love of God with a lost and dying world have both encouraged and humbled me.

I know Russ maybe more than most because we've stayed in each other's homes. We've traveled the world together and ministered side by side. And always he has demonstrated what the heart of Jesus is like. The only way to live like Jesus is to be continually filled with the Holy Spirit. ("Do not be drunk with wine but be continually filled with the Holy Spirit." Ephesians 5:18) And Pastor Russ epitomizes that.

To understand my personal perspective on Russ and his journey with the Holy Spirit let me share my own experience with a truly Spirit-filled person before I was born again myself. Coming from a nonreligious family, I was not convinced the story of Christ was real until I met some young people walking with the Holy Spirit like you walk with a friend.

I was an angry, rebellious young man when one of my best friends, who used LSD, called and asked if I wanted to do something really wild. Thinking it would be illegal, I said, "I'm in." His suggestion: go to church and make fun of the Christians. That sounded like fun. When we arrived, a 14-year-old girl came up to me, bold as brass, and told me three things no one in the world knew except me. She then proceeded to tell me a message from God. I had never seen anything like this. Little did we know there was a young American Baptist youth pastor who was training these kids to walk with the Holy Spirit.

From that day till the day I gave my life to Christ in 1969, I have learned tell the difference between Christians who could talk a good game and those who were filled with the Spirit of the living God. And I can tell you Russ is the real deal.

As a founder and senior pastor of a healthy church in upstate New York, I have had Russ in to minister for many years. Each time Russ visits I not only have him teach on the weekend but also have him minister to my leadership team. As he normally does, he has prayed over each leader, as well as the entire congregation, speaking prophetic words that only the Holy Spirit could give. Each time a prophetic word or a word of knowledge was given, people would receive healing in their souls.

When Russ ministers in China, India, Cuba, or any number of countries, he ministers from the same well he's learned to draw from, and that well is his relationship with the Holy Spirit.

I have walked with Jesus now for more than 48 years. I have been in Christian ministry for most of that time. I have helped plant six churches and traveled around the world meeting many strong believers who had amazing gifts and talents. But few of these people stack up to the character and gifting of Russ Frase.

If you want to learn from one of the best servants of God, read this book. If you want to know how to experience the power of the Holy Spirit in your own life, read this book. If you want to live the kind of Christian life that is described in the book of Acts, read this book.

Dale Jensen
Founder and Pastor Emeritus of Saratoga Abundant Life Church
Saratoga Springs, New York

Introduction

God has granted me the great privilege of ministering in 68 nations around the world during the last 50 years. In the process I have been blessed with several degrees, in ministry for 50 years with a wonderful wife and family. My life has been full and fruitful. As I have experienced these 74 years of life, I searched for and found purpose and true reality. There is the desire in every heart to be significant and to make a difference before the eventual day of departure. To live a life that is full and meaningful with peace, joy, and happiness is the quest of humanity.

This book is about finding that fulfillment in the joy of life through the purpose, work, and ministry of the Holy Spirit.

My desire is to candidly open my heart to you and share my journey and my experiences of half a century's walk with the Holy Spirit—sometimes struggles, sometimes great victories, and a lot of questions. My earnest hope and desire is that you will discover the rich depth of the Holy Spirit in every area of your life. And that you draw closer to Christ.

The Lord showed me something profound on a return flight from a missions trip overseas that spurred on the idea of *Runways of the Heart*, and ultimately, this book about my journey empowered by the Holy Spirit.

Dr. Russ Frase, Jr.

Former Dean of Rocky Mountain Bible Institute and

Founder of Joshua Nations in 2007

Flying Over the
Los Angeles Airport Runways

"Give Me complete access to the runways of your heart ..."

Flying into Los Angeles from overseas one night, coming down through the clouds, I marveled at the incredible lights of LA peering through the cloud layer—what a sight! As I saw the layout of runways, the Holy Spirit spoke to me.

> There are many runways down there to receive airplanes from all over the world. Without those runways planes could not land—planes that are carrying important cargo.
>
> It's the same with your heart. It is full of runways on which I desire to land My spiritual realities. I have so much for you, but if you don't allow Me access to the runways of your heart—arteries for vital life flow of My Spirit—I cannot fulfill my purposes, plans, and pleasures in your life.
>
> You must give Me complete access to the runways of your heart.
>
> If you do, you'll be amazed at the treasures I want to give you—the precious cargo I want to deliver to you. The wings of the Holy Spirit will fly the spiritual realities of the Father and Jesus into your heart. Surrender completely to Me and watch what we can do together.

Key Scripture Passages

John 16: 13-15, Acts 2:1-15, I Corinthians 12,
Romans 12:3-8, Ephesians 4:7-16, I Peter 4:10
(See Appendix C)

PART ONE
My Runways

CHAPTER 1
The Holy Spirit's Divine Detour

I sped in my SUV toward Denver International Airport, my mind reeling. Had I packed all I needed for two weeks of ministry in the Philippines?

Also, I couldn't stop thinking about my friend Dave Wurtsbaugh, fighting for his life in the Huntsman Cancer Institute in Salt Lake City. He had been a dear friend for many years and a true armor bearer. We had fought many spiritual battles together and traveled the world and ministered together. I loved him as a brother, and we both shared a deep passion and love for the Lord and for people.

Halfway to the airport, my cell phone rang.

"Pastor Russ, this is Roxi," Dave's wife said in a low trembling voice. "Dave is in really bad shape. His kidneys shut down, his temperature is 108 — when brain damage occurs — and his blood pressure has plummeted to dangerous levels. Doctors don't think he'll make it through the night."

My heart felt like it had torn to pieces. I needed to catch my plane to the Philippines in two hours, and my dear friend was at death's door. His wife stood watch alone at his bedside.

What should I do, Lord? I cried out in anguish. Then the Holy Spirit brought to my remembrance the story of Jesus who, while on His way to minister to someone in dire need, was interrupted by another who needed ministry.

I sensed His clear answer: *Go immediately to Salt Lake City.*

Yes, I need to reach my best bud! But how? I was five miles from the airport, with luggage to check and an international ticket in my pocket. How would

I make my connection so I could travel on to the Philippines in time to minister to Youth With A Mission (YWAM) students?

Call your son, I sensed that voice I'd become so familiar with tell me.

My son, Rusty, works for the airlines, which makes it possible to fly many of my trips around the world at no cost.

Surprisingly, he wasn't in the air somewhere and answered the phone. After I explained the situation, he said, "I'll see what I can do and call you right back."

Now two miles from the airport, I anxiously clutched my cell phone and almost dropped it when it rang.

"Dad, park and leave your luggage in the car. I booked a flight for you to Salt Lake City in two hours, returning tomorrow morning. I was also able to book a new flight to the Philippines. You'll still make it there on time."

"Thank you, Rusty!"

I wept as the burden fell from my shoulders and relief rushed in. *How perfect is the Holy Spirit, who knows what to do!* I'd obeyed Him, even though it seemed impossible. And He honored my willingness to do the right thing and put my friend's needs in front of a missions trip, even if I had to completely cancel it. I learned a lesson from the Lord that no mission is so important that you can't take care of a divine interruption.

At DIA, I hurriedly dialed Roxi's number. "I'm coming to you and Dave! Will you pick me up at the Salt Lake airport?"

In Utah, when she pulled to the airport curb, I looked into Roxi's eyes, and I could see her exhaustion from the long ordeal. I sent her to her hotel to rest. And I spent the night in the hospital room constantly praying in the Spirit for God to heal Dave's kidneys, for his body temperature to come down, and his blood pressure to come up. Off and on, I helped him out of bed to the restroom.

Then, in the morning, Roxi returned, and after I prayed with her, she took me back to the airport.

Before I boarded the plane for the Philippines, Roxi called my cell number. "Pastor Russ!" Her voice sounded bright. "Dave's kidneys are working, his blood pressure is normal, and his body temperature is normal! And you know what?" she added with a laugh. "Dave doesn't remember you came!"

I grinned. *Somehow it didn't matter.*

As I sank into my seat on the airplane, my heart burst with joy for the way the Holy Spirit had worked out all the details and allowed me to pray for Dave and still make it to the Philippines on time. I glanced out my small window at the crew as they scurried on the ground loading the plane with our suitcases and filling the tank with fuel.

I wept as memories swept over me—of Dave ministering with me in a dusty schoolroom in Pakistan, as we laughed at the practical jokes we played on each other, as we ate rubber chicken and saw the Holy Spirit set people free from bondages.

Thank you, Lord, for Your divine detour and for saving the life of my dear friend!

The jet engines roared, and we taxied and turned onto to the runway. With clearance from the air traffic control tower, the pilot skillfully picked up speed. I could imagine him with his copilot carefully monitoring the radar and listening to the radio frequency that guided him into the airspace reserved just for us.

I looked out my portal at the blue sky, the clouds, buildings, and houses below as they grew smaller and smaller while we climbed higher and higher. And the faces of the youth we'd be ministering to in the Philippines flashed in my mind and brought joy and peace.

I leaned back in the seat and closed my eyes with a smile, tears still brimming, knowing this is what God had prepared me for—taking off from this runway to soar and land across the ocean in my adventurous journey with the Holy Spirit. It was one of the most satisfying things in the world to me.

I eagerly looked forward to *more* of Him.

CHAPTER 2
Bad Boys

As Mom lay groaning in labor in the hospital bed, I beat my twin brother, Roy, out by a few minutes on April 24, 1944, in Fort Edward, New York. I never let him forget *I was first*. Well, actually sixth of seven kids. Rachel, Jim, Faith, Evie, Bob, me—but Roy was last.

My dad was a mild-mannered, short, bald-headed guy. When it came time to preach, he was very soft and gentle. All us kids and Mom attended church every Sunday morning, Sunday night, and Wednesday night.

But Roy and I were notoriously rebellious, even in our early elementary years. And the message didn't sink very far into our hearts. My mother had a hard time keeping up with all her children, and being the last of the litter, the two of us got away with a lot. We fidgeted and poked each other in church. And we paid little attention during the old Methodist tent revival meetings, but when they gave the altar call, we beelined for the front, afraid we'd go to hell. But we didn't make any commitment of the heart.

After I turned four, Dad was called to pastor in Vermont for three or four years, then we moved to upstate New York in Morley, a tiny town of 300 people near the Adirondack Mountains. There, Roy and I ran with a pack of boys who played football, baseball, and hockey together—and got into mischief. We loved climbing the bell tower of Dad's church with a bushel of rotten tomatoes and throwing them down on cars driving by.

Splat! Splat! Splat!

There wasn't much going on in that town. We had one firehouse, a one-room schoolhouse, and a lot of free time on our hands. On Saturday nights all the farmers congregated in a building in town to play pool. During the winter, with a fiercely warm cast iron furnace blazing, they opened the doors to let some heat out.

Huddled in the snow, heads together, snickering and plotting, my comrades and I packed snowballs and ran by, hurling them through the door and onto the pool table.

The farmers yelled and ran out the door after us, cussing and shaking their fists.

We also gathered firecrackers and hung around outside the general store across from the parsonage where my family lived. The guy who ran the store owned a little black-and-white TV set—one of the few sets in the town. During boxing season on Saturday nights, the farmers gathered around that blinking screen, shouting and screaming at the slicked-up, muscled-up guys in the ring.

Outside with my pack, I whistled quietly and looked down the street to make sure the coast was clear. Then I gave the signal, and Paul lit the cracker and punched it through the keyhole.

BANG!

We ran like crazy while those farmers hurled open the door and rushed onto the street, cussing and hollering again. Four blocks away, we finally stopped and rolled on the ground laughing and hooting and slapping one another.

Another favorite: We'd place a burlap bag alongside one of the streets with some potatoes rolling out of the mouth of the sack. Unwary drivers would see the bag and stop to pick it up. As they reached down to pick it up, it would mysteriously fly out of their hands. My mischievous friends and I had tied it to a rope and were hiding in some bushes along the road. They'd curse, and we'd scream in delight from our hideaway!

That trick brought us so much fun.

Until one night, after we jerked the sack, we peered around the bush to see the red face of a state trooper in his headlights glaring in our direction. We ran away as fast as we could, but he caught us.

I remember clearly the whipping Roy and I got from that one.

As you can tell, I didn't relate to my mom and dad's stuffy religion. There were so many *don'ts,* and I had a lot of *doing* in me.

Work and Play

Despite all this mischief, I developed a good work ethic. Starting at age 8, I mowed lawns for 25 cents an hour. Dad's salary was only $37.50 a week, which didn't come close to supporting nine people, so all of us worked hard planting, weeding, and harvesting our food from three gardens on the land next to the parsonage. We milked a cow, took care of chickens, and slopped the hogs.

The family moved to Cobleskill, New York, when Roy and I turned 13. Our eighth grade summer, we ramped up our fun in a whole new way. One hot day while diving and splashing at the old swimming hole with our friends, the kids from the community college showed up and took over. They brought Genesee beer, offering my friends and me our first cans of beer. From then on, we couldn't get enough of that happy-time alcoholic buzz.

Throughout my high school years during the summer, we baled hay eight hours a day and loaded it on trucks. Our old farmer friend paid us each $8 cash at the end of the day. With the cash in our pockets, we went barhopping, hung out behind the high school, and drank ourselves silly. The next day, we loaded up the truck and headed out and baled hay. Hung over and throwing up, we vowed we'd never do it again. But by nighttime, we caroused again in the bars.

Roy and I ran in different circles in high school. Both of us loved sports. He wrestled. I ran cross-country track and played on the basketball team. Our basketball team went undefeated for three years while I played, and we won several state titles. The name of the team was the Red Devils. Maybe that's why Dad wouldn't come to the basketball games!

My pals and I were particularly bored one summer night. "Hey, I've got an idea," I told them. "When my dad goes to sleep, let's roll the car out of the garage. I know where the key is."

Seven of my jock friends agreed this was a great idea, so in the dark, we pushed Dad's '58 Pontiac onto the driveway, piled in, and I drove us, yelling and whooping, to one of our favorite bars. In the dark, smoky room we flirted with the girls and got rip-roaring drunk.

"Hey, do ya think it's time to leave yet?" one guy said, as he tried to sit on a barstool but fell to the ground.

Another friend standing next to him laughed loudly, and in slow motion he picked up my friend. "Well, I'm not ready, but you sure are! Maybe we'd better go."

They looked at me and the other guys sitting at a table. I downed my beer, took one last look at the pretty girls coyly smiling at us from a nearby table, and pulled the keys out of my pocket. "Okay, guess we've got to have our priorities—baling hay in the morning."

The guys around me laughed, then staggered to their feet. With a wink at the girls, my hand almost missed the doorknob on the way out. It didn't occur to me that I might not be in any condition to drive.

We left the bar singing and bouncing along on the rambling country road as the rancid smell of beer choked the tiny inside of the car. Curve ahead—I almost missed it. I turned my steering wheel just in time.

Screeeeeeech! I hit my brakes as the guardrail for a bridge loomed in front of us. We were going too fast. I turned one way, almost hitting the rail on the wrong side of the road, then overcorrected. My mind willed my hand to *turn, turn the steering wheel back,* but it was too late. We crashed through the edge of the bridge and kept going right into a corn silo on the other side. And stopped. Halfway in, and halfway out of the silo with corn piling on top of and around the car.

"Ughhhh!" Low moans and groans sounded all around me.

"Excuse me, sir." A patrolman tapped on my window, flashlight shining in my eyes. "Are you all okay?"

As I rolled down the window a crack, I'm sure he got a whiff of the alcohol oozing out of all of us. I looked at his face in the moonlight and saw a flicker of recognition. I recognized him, too. Wasn't this Officer Martin, a die-hard fan of the Red Devils? Hadn't I seen him clapping and yelling at us from the stands during many of our games?

I don't know how it happened, but we didn't get a ticket. We didn't even get a reprimand. I can't even remember having a conversation with our parents. I don't know how Dad afforded to buy a new car, but that problem sank to the back of my mind when basketball season started again.

We can block the runways that will take us to our God-purposed destinations. It is our choice. I blocked mine. One Saturday night I got very drunk and crashed into bed. The next morning before church, my pastor dad came upstairs and compassionately put his hand on my arm and asked if he could pray for me. I angrily shoved him away. He offered me freedom, but rejecting him, I chose bondage.

A bondage that spiraled me downward into a life of loneliness and destruction.

CHAPTER 3
Drunk

In 1963, after I graduated high school, I hitchhiked to a little college in Missouri carrying a satchel with tuna fish sandwiches and chocolate chip cookies. Wanting to make it on my own, I patted my pocket with $15 in it. Later, I found a little Bible my mama had snuck into my satchel, which I opened and read every now and then.

But not too often.

While I attended Central Missouri State Teachers College in Warrensburg, I stayed drunk for almost two-and-one-half years. To earn money, I ironed shirts in the dorm for 25 cents a shirt, and by the time the weekend rolled around, I had enough cash for my friends and me to get plastered. I lived a never-ending treadmill of futility and loneliness, even in a crowd.

I was looking for something more, something to fill a huge empty place in my soul.

Finally fed up with the endless cycle of drinking, carousing, studying, bartending, and pointless partying, I threw my few belongings into a duffel bag and left for my sister and brother-in-law's home in Lafayette, Indiana. Dick and Rachel Bower took me in. And a nightclub owner hired me. Unaware of the circumstances lining up around me, I became a crackerjack bartender by night and managed a cafeteria during the day.

How often do we think we are moving toward happiness, but in truth, our direction is toward brokenness? Even in my brokenness God cared for me and reached out to me in many ways. Little did I know God set me up.

It started a few years earlier with a 39-cent Sears catalog. Deep in the heart of the South in Alabama, a man hoping to earn a good living for his wife and three kids bought a kit from the catalog and soon learned how to wire homes. As the years rolled by, one of his daughters graduated from International Bible College while I attended the teachers' college in Missouri.

A contractor influential in the man's life called one day. "Hey! Have I got a great job for you!"

"Yeah? What?"

"Wiring a basketball arena. In Indiana! For Purdue University."

"You are kidding."

Erskine Lowery moved his family from Tuscumbia, Alabama, to Indiana.

While I managed the cafeteria, the strip center merchants came to the cafeteria for coffee and pastries. One morning, in walked a tall, slender knockout wearing a miniskirt and a mohair sweater.

I found out later, she sold shoes a few doors down, a holiday in-between job.

"I'm Going to Marry That Man! But First Get Him Saved …"

Lana, the daughter of the electrician who'd moved several states away and wired the Purdue stadium, stole my heart.

Later, I asked Paul, who worked with Lana, "Does she have a boyfriend?"

"I don't think so."

I hemmed and hawed a bit. But my desire outweighed my awkwardness. "Would you ask her if she'd go see Ray Charles with me at Purdue?" I didn't quite have the guts to ask her myself.

When he asked Lana, she said she already had a date that night. I gave the tickets away, went out, and got drunk as usual.

But I was not going to give up. Within a week, I'd conjured up another idea for a date. Dinner and entertainment at Arnie's Pizza Parlor.

After we settled at a table, I took a gulp of my beer and a drag on my cigarette while two of the raunchiest comedians I'd heard in a long time told their off-color jokes.

"So … what do you like to do?" I asked Lana.

"Go to church."

I gulped. *What's a nice Christian girl doing with a pagan like me?* I wondered. But as I sat at that table with her, I knew in my heart that I was going to marry her. You see, no matter what path we take in life, God is always hunting us and wants to capture our hearts. He captured my heart using this "Alabama Knockout."

Lana told me later that she went home that night and told her sister, "I'm going to marry that Yankee boy, Russ."

Scowling, Barbara replied, "What do you mean, marry him? You don't even know him."

Lana flung herself onto the couch and kicked off her high heels. "Well, I'll get him *cleaned up* first."

Beer in the Afternoon, Church in the Evening

Lana and I became inseparable, and we went everywhere together. I was still drinking and smoking. A mutual friend of ours approached Lana and asked her, "Would you help Russ? He's on his way to becoming an alcoholic, and he's too nice a guy for that."

She wasn't sure how she could help. "I guess I could invite him to church."

So she took me on as a "case" and invited me to her Baptist church one Sunday night. I had to drink a six-pack Sunday afternoon before I could get up the courage to go. But that's about as far as it went. The congregation could smell me ten pews away! But I went so I could sit close to and put my arm around that beautiful woman. Though it was *wun-der-ful* going to church with her, it's the only reason I went—to be with Lana.

When the pastor gave an altar call, I'd get up and walk out the door and smoke a Marlboro on the front steps.

A couple of elderly ladies in the church realized how important I was to Lana and took me on as their case, too. I heard later they prayed for me all the time.

Got My Ticket before "Flight Final"

This cycle of drinking, smoking, working, and going to church with Lana on Sunday nights went on for six months. But something was slowly eating away at me, changing the way I saw things, and I realized something was wrong. One Wednesday evening, the pastor played a 78 rpm record called "Flight Final." It was the story of taking the final flight to heaven, and you'd better get your ticket. When they turned the record over, the words from the hymn "I'll Meet You in the Morning" seeped into a long-ago forgotten place in my memory, reminding me of my mom humming that tune.

> *I'll meet you in the morning by the bright riverside,*
> *when all sorrow has drifted away;*
> *I'll be standing at the portals when the gates open wide*
> *at the close of that long weary day.*
> *… you'll know me in the morning by the smile that I wear …*

I pictured Mom with her well-earned white hair tied up in what we call a "glory knot" and realized that night I wasn't going to meet her—or *anybody*—in heaven because I wouldn't be going there. Something turned in my heart for the first time since those Methodist tent revival days. My heart churned as Holy Spirit conviction fell. It dawned on me—*really* dawned on me.

I am lost. I am a sinner, separated from a personal relationship with God. If I am going to be "born again," I need to open my heart and let Christ in.

Up until now, I'd tried to fill my emptiness and dull my fears and lone-liness with a different kind of spirit—booze—but when the buzz wore off, the desolate feelings remained. In that moment, like a misty fog lifting from a hidden farm pond, I realized the only way out of this never-ending cycle that spiraled me downward, and the only way I'd experience eternal life with God in heaven, was to accept Christ into my life.

As this realization penetrated deep into my heart, while I stood next to Lana, I surrendered my life to the God I'd been running away from for a long time. A heavy burden I'd been dragging around dropped from my shoulders in that moment. The power of the Word and the Holy Spirit invaded one of the lonely hearts: mine. God taught me, a sinner, in the way, and my heart's conscience cried out about right and wrong. And, He used a 78 record, which I still have in the bookcase behind me in my study reminding me of that special night five decades ago.

It seems like I floated to the front of the church to acknowledge I had just received Christ in my heart. No doubt about it, I'd finally found the answer for me. I believed in the righteousness of God in my heart first, then I walked down the aisle giving my hand to the preacher and making confession with my lips that Jesus would now be the Lord of my life. I knew the journey of my old life was over and my new journey with Jesus was beginning. No tears, no emotions, but as rock-solid genuine as one could be.

God has special ways to reach us, even if they are unconventional. Lana had a hard time believing my decision was for real. But when she saw what God did for me—I was totally delivered from smoking and drinking that night—she knew that was not something I could have done on my own. She realized her prayers, and those of her little old lady friends in the church, had been answered.

But Lana didn't count on me suddenly getting so radical. I sensed God calling me to preach as soon as I got saved, but I didn't tell her for several months. Smart move. She was grateful I'd become a Christian, but she was not interested in marrying a preacher. She'd known a lot of unhappy pastors' wives. She later told others, "You couldn't *pay* me to marry a pastor!" She was okay with me getting involved in the jail ministry at the church. In fact, she joined a group that visited the jail with me.

But that's as far as she wanted to go.

Call to Preach and to the Ministry

As a good Baptist new believer, I quickly agreed to teach junior high kids in Sunday school the next week. Standing before the group, I asked myself, *What am I doing here?* And then I heard the whisper of the Holy Spirit, *There's more …there's more …*

I didn't think that *more* was in the classroom at Purdue University, but nevertheless I continued to pursue a bachelor's degree. One day, sinking into the large, green overstuffed chair in our living room, my eyes fell on an article in the newspaper and a picture of empty-eyed prisoners looking through the bars in their cells. The caption mentioned no clergy had visited them during the Christmas holidays.

A very strong impression came to me. *I want you to go to the jail and speak to these men.*

I stood up and looked in the living room mirror, perplexed. *Me?*

Yes—you!

I walked into the bedroom and around the house trying to figure out what was happening. I went back to the living room, sat down, opened the paper to the story again, and that same strange impression came to me. *Go and speak to the men.*

Bewildered, I called my pastor, Jesse James Buell, and told him what had happened.

"This is amazing," he said. "Our head deacon was just in my office, and he said, 'Pastor, we need to start up our jail ministry again, but we don't have a preacher.'"

Dumbfounded by the timing, we connected the dots of the leading of the Holy Spirit, and I soon showed up at the jail, Bible in hand.

This was my call to preach the gospel of the kingdom, 50 years ago. (It is that same call that feeds and fuels everything ahead for each of us.)

An odd sense came over me when I preached my first sermon, "The Jailhouse Rock," about Paul and Silas in jail praising God when an earthquake shook them loose from their chains. As I held my Bible and spoke to them about how much God loved them and had a special purpose in each of their lives, my heart overflowed with passion for the gospel. Disappointingly, looking back at me was a cluster of semi-repentant guys.

That soft, still voice sounded in my heart again, *There's* more. *More* of what, I wasn't sure. But a hunger gnawed at me during the next few months for more of *something*.

Wedding

Lana and I married on June 1, 1968. Since Indiana was far from upstate New York and Deep South Alabama, the only family able to come were my sister and brother-in-law. As we stood together in that simple ceremony in the beautiful little Methodist church Lana had chosen, I had no clue about marriage or what I was doing other than loving Lana. Our only preparation was a book the pastor gave us, which we were too busy to read. Love is gloriously blind.

I continued to attend Purdue University while I worked at Alcoa. Lana stayed at the shoe store, stocking up on her shoe collection at discount prices.

A year after I embraced Christ, I discovered what the voice that whispered *Something more* might have meant.

CHAPTER 4
A Different Kind of Drunk

Zealous in my new faith, in my new walk, in the Word of God, and in my new call, I was learning to have an intimate relationship with Jesus. I sensed I'd need the help of someone who knew Him better than I did—the Holy Spirit. One of His roles is to reveal Jesus to us in more detail. John 14 defines this for us where Jesus says He does not leave us as orphans (that is, somebody who is unrelated or disconnected from God). The Holy Spirit, our guide and counselor, knows everything about Jesus and will reveal Him to us in all His splendor if we will only ask.

I began to encounter a deeper work of the Spirit in some unexpected ways. Lana's mom, Clovie, invited us to a small Bible study—a life group—in her home. Her red-haired preacher walked through the door and said matter-of-factly, "Nobody will be able to survive in the coming days without the baptism of the Holy Spirit."

The hairs on the back of my neck stood up. *I got it all when I was born again. Who is this guy to tell us we need a baptism of the Holy Spirit?*

Another time soon after I was saved, Clovie took Lana and me to a Pentecostal church service. As we arrived, nuns and priests, some playing guitars, sashayed on the stage to "He brought me to the banqueting table; His banner over me was love …" We found seats, but I couldn't keep my eyes off them—it wasn't so much what they were singing, but the powerful presence of *liquid love* that flowed all over the stage as they swished their robes like brooms cleaning a kitchen. It filled the atmosphere with a warmth that moved and melted my heart. I'd never experienced anything like this.

I don't understand. What in the world is going on here? I had been broken for so long, so hungry and thirsty, like the woman at the well in John 4. When this woman, who had had five husbands, and the one she was living with was not hers, was so thirsty for true reality of happiness, joy and peace, and significance. She was so broken but becomes whole.

Settling back into my seat next to Lana, I felt surges of unseen power in their movements. I admitted, *There's more about God that I don't know.* I'd learned a lot about Jesus and was gaining skills in studying the Bible. I knew some things about the Father, but didn't know what the person, work, and ministry of the Holy Spirit was.

I sensed that something was going to change in my spiritual journey, though I couldn't quite put my finger on what.

Youth Revival in Corban, Kentucky

In September 1969, a year and three months after Lana and I were married, my chance to see the work of the Holy Spirit came in an unusual and unexpected way. A pastor just out of seminary invited me to preach at a youth revival in the coal-mining town of Corban, Kentucky. I walked through the big double doors of this dignified Southern Baptist church and stepped on deep red, plush carpeting.

I preached that night like the wild man I was—at my first youth revival. I was so young and green behind the ears—a rookie with the Redeemer's love.

After preaching the message, I gave an invitation to the youth to come to the altar. And I encouraged their parents to come with them and pray for their kids. When none of the parents joined us, I didn't know what to do. It was awkward—the service was over. But something stirred, and I wanted to keep a hold on it.

I turned to a couple of teenagers and asked, "Is there a room where we can go?" They led me and their friends to a back room, where we joined the pastor. I looked around at the room full of kids, some on their knees, faces on the carpeting, some looking upward with tears streaming down their faces. They were confessing sins to one another, asking for forgiveness from each other.

The pastor knelt in a corner, his eyes closed as his black-rimmed glasses slipped down on his face. He seemed lost in another dimension. One young teenage girl sat on a table, crying out to God. It seemed to me she'd reached into heaven and brought the presence of Jesus right down into the room. I remember it even today.

What in the world is happening here? I don't have a clue ...

And then it happened! That *more* I had been searching for came in a new reality. The Holy Spirit, like a 747 jet, flew in from above and landed on the runways of my heart. Let me quickly say that when I was born again, I was baptized into the Body of Christ, placed into the family of God with salvation and all that it affords. But I could tell this was a fresh infilling, baptizing work of the Holy Spirit. An incredible joy consumed me as I took a few weaving steps. I'd been drunk more times than I'd wanted to remember in various bars. But this was a *good drunk,* with joy unspeakable and full of glory (and a 50-year hangover, I might add). Like I'd just downed a large Holy Spirit drink.

I'd asked the Lord to fill me in a deeper way, and an overwhelming sense of how much God loved me and a love for others I'd never previously experienced overcame me. Nobody told me a relationship with Christ could fill every cell in my body with such a strong presence like this. This young pastor and teens were on to something. The Lord baptized me with love, understanding, and the gift of evangelist that night, alongside a new love for Jesus that would cement my relationship with Him and service in His kingdom.

As full as I was, my heart hungered for even *more* of the Holy Spirit and a deeper understanding of the things of the Spirit. I would soon learn there is *more*, much *more*. The voice of the Holy Spirit is so good to guide us in the eternal truths and receive the things of the Father and Jesus. And today, as I write more than five decades later, I continue to hear the voice of the Holy Spirit in new ways. You see, He never stops speaking to us, but many times we are not listening. And when we do hear Him, we must yield the runways of our heart to Him.

Upon every runway we open up to Him, He will land his precious cargo. I was only beginning to understand what some of that cargo could be.

CHAPTER 5
First Things First

New experiences of life began to shape Lana and our new family, ones that would help us navigate the journey by listening to the Holy Spirit. It would be more than a whisper but a voice we could trust and relate to. Learning to trust does not always make things easy, but it is right. We learned the Holy Spirit is a comforter; He is God at hand in every step we took.

John 14:16: "And I will pray the Father, and He will give you another Helper, that He may abide with you forever."

Our First Child and Our First Church

Lana delivered our firstborn, Paula Michelle, in Lafayette, Indiana, on June 7, 1970. What joy she brought into our lives! We put her bed in the closet of our one-bedroom apartment—the only place we could find. Although she slept in a little room, she took up a large place in our hearts.

I graduated from Purdue University with a bachelor of arts degree in December 1972. Casting my net for good seminaries, I chose Southwestern Baptist Theological Seminary in Fort Worth, Texas, for my pastoral training. We moved our little family across country so I could start in January 1973. Lana loved the fact that I didn't preach at the church we chose to attend, and we could sit side by side, enjoying the message together.

One day during my first semester of school, one of my seminary professors pulled me aside. "Russ, how would you like to fill in and preach at a little country church next Sunday?" The church often brought in seminary students.

"I'd love to!"

I preached in the Virginia Hills Baptist Church for several weeks and found out they were "trying out" two other seminary students to fill the role of pastor.

I told them in order to be fair to all of us they needed to make a decision between us.

So they chose me.

Now we have a problem, I thought. *Lana doesn't want to be a pastor's wife.* She had not gone with me to any of the services.

I realized God had to speak to her, because I didn't have enough influence at this time to change her heart.

"Honey, this Sunday the deacons in Virginia Hills Baptist Church want to vote on whether to bring me aboard as pastor of their church," I told Lana one day as 4-year-old Paula tugged on her top while she stirred our dinner. She had not joined me at the church until now, but to my surprise, in her fiercely loyal way, she declared, "They've never met me, and they are going to vote on whether you will be their pastor? Not going to happen without me checking them out!"

On Sunday morning, my wife and daughter rode with me to the church. My heart sang the whole way because Lana came with me this time.

We drove over rolling hills past cow pastures, country farmhouses, and feed silos and finally arrived at the white clapboard church sitting on a hill under fragrant pine trees. A postcard perfect scene. Warm country folks, mostly older farmhands, greeted the three of us at the door with bright smiles on their sun-wrinkled faces. We stepped into the small sanctuary that could accommodate 125 people, with its wooden pews and stand-alone small pulpit and hidden baptistery.

"I really love that church and the people there!" Lana told me later. She rejoiced when they voted me in. We traveled back and forth from Fort Worth to the church on weekends for more than two years. And while I pastored that tiny congregation, we enjoyed many invitations to peoples' homes for dinner after Sunday service (a true blessing for this seminary student's family), the fellowship, and the many gospel sing-alongs and special events. They organized delicious family potlucks overflowing with farm fresh homemade comfort foods like roast beef, fresh garden vegetables, turnip greens, and hot apple pies.

In March 1974, we moved into the little parsonage down the hill in Athens. It was small but cozy for our small family of three—and one on the way.

Missed Opportunities

June 20, 1974. "I think it's time." Lana rubbed her belly as Russell Weldon Frase III kicked her. I grabbed her suitcase, and we rushed out the door and into our car. After settling her in the hospital room, I remembered how Paula took her time—24 hours—before coming into the world.

I'll bet this kid will take a while. So I'll go home and get my seminary books and study while I'm waiting.

When I got on the elevator, I noticed a very tall, astute-looking man with sideburns, jaw set resolutely, standing with his arms folded. I thought, *Gee, he looks familiar.*

As I stepped off the elevator and the doors clanged shut, I realized, *That was Billy Graham! I just missed the opportunity of a lifetime!* Here I was a seminary student standing a foot away from this world-famous preacher. He must have been making hospital rounds. What seminarian wouldn't have died to see Billy Graham? And we didn't even talk.

When I returned to the hospital after retrieving my books, Lana had delivered Rusty.

Like a Singer Sewing Machine

Dave Barclay, a friend of mine, and I surrendered to preach the same night in the Creasey Lane Baptist Church in Lafayette, Indiana, in 1968. His father was one of the spiritual leaders in the Southern Baptist Convention in that county. Then Dave took off for school in Missouri. I continued at Purdue. We later heard that Dave had gotten messed up with those "tongue-talkers." Though this wasn't Baptist practice and policy, it didn't bother me that *others* held those beliefs. My introduction into that world at Lana's mom's Pentecostal church with the sashaying nuns and the life group had opened the door to that world a crack.

Dave and I reunited at Southwestern Seminary.

One Friday night, as I collated forms coming off the press in the print shop where I worked, I sensed God speaking to me, *Tonight is your night.*

My night? I wondered what that meant.

I finished my jobs and arrived home to a joyous welcome from Lana.

"Boy, I wish you could have heard Andre Crouch tonight!" Lana exclaimed, dropping into our comfy chair and kicking off her heels. "It was a great concert. Dave, Bonnie, and I really enjoyed it."

We heard an urgent rap on the door.

"Who in the world could that be?" I opened it to my friend Dave's smiling face as he pushed his way in.

"I have to tell you what great things I've experienced with the Holy Spirit!" he exclaimed, making himself at home on the couch.

I stiffened. "Look," I said to him curtly. "I am a good Baptist boy—like *you* were once! I don't need this. I've got all of the Holy Spirit I need."

As I said that, the vision of that girl in the church in Corban, Kentucky, sitting on a table with tears streaming down her face and a radiant presence all around her flashed in my mind. I saw her again pulling heaven down into the room and the words *something more …something more* tugged at my heart.

Dave sensed my hungry heart. "You can have more …"

Why did he have to put it that way?

Lana watched us from her comfy spot, almost like we were an entertaining sideshow. We'd been going on for hours and now it was 4 a.m.—almost time to greet a new day.

"It's very easy," Dave said. "Here's all we need to do."

I slid to my knees, overwhelmed with the presence of God, and bowed my head. "Okay, Lord, I surrender to You. Fill me with Your Spirit."

Dave put his hand on my shoulder and began quietly praying in a different language. Instead of seeming so weird, at that moment it was beautiful to me, like God Himself was speaking a message from heaven. I felt a kind of bubbling up inside my belly.

"Just praise him," Dave said. "In English. Or if you hear another language, just speak that out."

Surprised, I did hear another language deep inside me. It began to bubble out, and I began to speak it. More and more, this language flowed out of me. Out of the corner of my eye, I caught Lana watching me with rapt attention, a smile on her face. More of these words came until I sounded like my mom's old singer sewing machine.

Dave turned to Lana. "Do you want the baptism of the Holy Spirit?"

Lana was hesitant and curious but wanted to watch me because she knew I would not do anything unbiblical or foolish. (She later received the infilling of the Holy Spirit in the quiet of our bedroom.)

I have learned through the years that the Holy Spirit deals with each of us in accordance to our experiences, our personalities, our openness, or our close-mindedness. He is the same Holy Spirit, but we all respond differently. He releases Himself to us in many different ways (1 Corinthians 12:4–7).

On that evening with Dave Barclay, I broke through the fear barrier of the spiritual unknown into a faith blessing of greater depth in Christ. The Holy Spirit landed a planeload of spiritual realities, riches that I am still mining (2 Timothy 1:7). I found the better freedom to be released into the Spirit of God. Where the Spirit of the Lord is, there is liberty.

My Dilemma

The next day, I knew I had a big problem. Here I was going to the citadel of Baptist theology at Southwestern Seminary and pastoring a Baptist church. *What am I going to do?* The Baptist Convention was expelling churches that were infiltrated with "wild" teachings on the power gifts of the Spirit, especially those that practiced speaking in tongues. Some of the leaders declared this practice was of the devil. Or the more "learned" scholars dismissed it as something that ended with the era of the Apostles and the New Testament church—the teaching of cessationism. Some of the students quietly slipped off to charismatic churches, without letting their professors know.

> The Holy Spirit will always give instruction along with what He does. He is the greatest teacher. He was schooled in the heart of God and Jesus. He has been here before the foundations of the world, He and the Father and Jesus planning the scenarios of God just for you and me.

Now, here I was in a terrible fix—speaking in tongues, with new revelation, actually pastoring a Southern Baptist church where this was not accepted.

Lord, what am I going to do?

I sensed His answer. *Keep your mouth shut.*

That sounded like a very good idea to me.

But the truth of it gnawed at the depths of my soul.

So I began my quest for more of the presence of God. I cried out to the Holy Spirit to help me and teach me about what had just happened.

One day on my way to class, as I crossed the seminary commons, I heard a condemning voice, *That's you doing this, not God.*

I said, "You are right! It is me, with my new prayer language, a new spiritual language. Three days ago I didn't have it, but today I do."

I learned that day not to let the devil talk me out of what God has done in me. Satan will always challenge what the Holy Spirit gives. Fear, the unknown, opinions of others—these can clog up the runways of our hearts and keep us from taking off into the divine destiny God has for us.

A new expression of heaven downloaded into my spirit being. And a new dimension of *more* was about to invade my life.

CHAPTER 6
Déjà Vu

The week after my middle-of-the-night argument with Dave, wrestling with God and surrendering to the Spirit, I had an open vision, something I found out later occurs when we are awake. This was the first open vision I'd ever had.

As Lana and I stepped out of the doorway of our parsonage to walk up the hill to the Sunday morning service, I saw in a vision a young man in khaki pants and a light blue shirt, with a headful of blond hair, walking up the aisle at our church. He looked like he was perhaps in his early 30s.

We went up the hill to get to our beautiful country church, breathing in the fresh pine scents, looking out on miles of rolling hills and fields.

I totally forgot about what I'd seen by the time we sang our three hymns, passed the offering plate, and I'd delivered my sermon. After I gave an invitation at the end, a young man in his 30s in khaki pants, a light blue shirt, and with blond hair came walking up the aisle toward me ready to accept Jesus into his heart. It startled me. I hadn't even seen him in the service.

He was one of the country boys everyone knew.

First Word of Knowledge

There are many new firsts in the filling work of the Holy Spirit. The word of knowledge was a first for me. The word of knowledge is receiving information we could not know any other way but by the Holy Spirit. It is insider information.

As a busy seminary student and Lana with her hands full with two young children at home, we loved the invitations we'd receive for dinner on Sundays after church. Those country ladies could really cook up a meal, and they loved to invite the preacher over. Those were the days when you freely visited peoples' homes, and even in the confines of Baptist theology, we had a lot of fun and freedom.

And every fifth Sunday, the church celebrated Fifth Sunday Dinner on the Grounds. It was a bountiful church potluck overflowing with food and fellowship. Boy, they packed it in!

After the dinner, we'd have a gospel singing service from 2 to 4 p.m. Three or four local groups would come and belt out that good ole gospel music!

One Sunday, we'd finished dinner and moved into the sanctuary to enjoy the music. Lana and I were sitting on the front row as one of the groups filed up to the front. As they began to sing, a distinct thought came into my mind: *See that lead singer? This is going to be her last performance.*

What? Where's that coming from?

I looked around. Everyone seemed to be enjoying the gospel group and oblivious to the conversation I seemed privy to.

I wondered half to myself, *Why is this going to be her last performance?*

She has a condition in her throat, and she's very discouraged. She wants to quit.

I couldn't shake this strong impression that someone was telling me this specific information—information about this lady that no one else, including myself, knew. The voice sounded familiar.

Stand up after she finishes singing and tell her what I just told you. And tell her not to quit.

I slunk down in my chair and glanced around at the oblivious crowd. *You've got to be kidding! Is this you, Lord?*

That sense of peace and rightness that overcomes a person when you-know-that-you-know-that-you-nailed-it filled me. *Well, that's nice, Lord. Thanks for letting me know. But I'm not going to do it. I'm not going to make a fool of myself and spout something that is just something I'm making up in my head. What would they think of me? Brother Frase, Southern Baptist pastor, seminary boy …?*

The upbeat melody of the song crowded out my anxious thoughts, and I joined the audience clapping the beat to the rousing chorus.

When they finish singing, I want you to stand up and tell her.

It seemed pretty clear to me by now that this must be the Lord, but I continued to argue with Him. *Well, they aren't going to finish. I have to go to the radio station to produce my program soon.*

Suddenly, the lady hit her last powerful note and ended the song to a loud cheering crowd. Almost as though I were a puppet and the master pulled my strings and picked me up out of my chair, I stood and spoke in front of God and all the Baptists.

"This is going to be your last service," I said to the lady—and to all the faces that suddenly swiveled in my direction. "You are thinking of quitting. I want to encourage you to not quit, but continue singing." I mentioned nothing about the growth in her throat. Much safer. *Too much information.*

I hurried away from the service to the radio station and conducted my regular Sunday afternoon preaching program.

Later at home, after Lana and I put the kids to bed, Lana said, "You know, Janet came up to me afterwards and told me, 'What your husband said is true. But what he didn't mention was that I have a physical growth in my throat.'"

That stunned me. In my personal Bible study time, I'd read about a gift of the Spirit that God sometimes gives to His children. "To another [is given] the **word of knowledge** through the same Spirit" (1 Corinthians 12:8).

I had been afraid to mention the growth in her throat. I kicked myself for not telling her that but learned a great lesson that day. The Holy Spirit had released a spiritual gift called a word of knowledge—a true fact I didn't know with my natural senses—through me to confirm what was going on in her life and to encourage her to keep singing.

Not understanding what God is doing and making mistakes is all a part of the learning process as we grow in the spiritual gifts. This incident was just a beginning of that spiritual gift operation in my life. I knew then that I had so much to learn in this new spiritual realm.

Despite the growing uncertainty about all that was taking place in my life, I eagerly accepted this new word to me in the things of the Spirit. The good truth is that the Holy Spirit and the Word of God will teach us. We often fear what will happen to our reputations, what will others think and wonder, *what if it isn't the Lord?* These types of fears and thoughts keep many from moving into spiritual experiences.

I was beginning to understand this is the way the Holy Spirit works. He makes things happen and lets us be a part. He can show us everything we need to know about our lives, the lives of people, the future, what's going to happen in any dimension, on any level in the world. He will reveal what we need to know when we need to know it, and He has the ability to show us what He knows before we need to know it. Jesus said He would take the things of God and show them to us (John 16:14). Oftentimes, we don't realize how blessed we are.

With experiences in 68 nations and decades later, I've learned we have so much available to us in the Holy Spirit if we will just open new runways in our hearts—move out the heavy equipment that clutter our current runways for the new spiritual realities of God. First Corinthians 2:9–10 says, "Eye has not seen, nor ear heard, nor have entered into the heart of man the things that God has prepared for those who love him. But God has revealed them to us through his Spirit."

It is one of the roles of the Holy Spirit to reveal to us what our natural eyes have not seen, what our natural ears have not heard, and what our natural minds have never imagined. The revealing power of the Holy Spirit is like opening shades with sunlight pouring into a dark room where things that were hidden before can now be clearly seen. In the same way the Holy Spirit's revelation and workings in our lives drives out spiritual darkness and gives daylight clarity on a situation, a problem needing to be solved, a direction He wants us to go, or a wonderful truth about Jesus. Jesus reveals who the Father is, and the Holy Spirit reveals to us Jesus, which is one of His greatest works.

Acts 2:17–21 repeats what Joel says in the Old Testament:

> And it shall come to pass in the last days, says God,
> That I will pour out of My Spirit on all flesh;
> Your sons and your daughters shall prophesy,
> Your young men shall see visions,
> Your old men shall dream dreams.
>
> And on My menservants and on My maidservants
> I will pour out My Spirit in those days;
> And they shall prophesy.
>
> I will show wonders in heaven above
> And signs in the earth beneath:

Blood and fire and vapor of smoke.

The sun shall be turned into darkness,
And the moon into blood,
Before the coming of the great and awesome day of the Lord.

And it shall come to pass
That whoever calls on the name of the Lord
Shall be saved.

I believe we are in those last days. We may fear the unknown, but I assure you that when we open our hearts to the treasures of these gifts He wants to bestow on us, He'll use us in great and mighty ways beyond what we could have even imagined—and accurately reveal to us His great mysteries.

CHAPTER 7

Lady Delivered
from 13 Demons

At the end of the summer not long after God gave me my first vision (the country boy in the khaki pants) and my first prophetic word (encouragement to the gospel singer), a weird thing happened. After a revival service in our little country church, I gave an invitation at the altar for people to accept Jesus into their hearts. Several people bunched up in front of me, crying, praying, and repenting of their sins.

Arrrrrrrrr! Arrrrrrr!

The sound startled me, and I surveyed the group to figure out where it was coming from. A woman in the crowd around me raised her hands over her contorted face, red hair flying everywhere. People moved out of the way, but strangely, they resumed their kneeling penitent prayers in a semicircle around her.

Arrrrrr! Ohhhhh!

I looked into her reddened face, wondering what could be causing such agony. *Now what do I do?*

Nobody else seemed to know. I mean, this was quite unusual for a Southern Baptist church in those days.

Then a brilliant idea came to me. I turned to her husband, a big man clad in farmer's overalls, and he looked perplexed. "Go ahead and take her home. And call me if you need me."

I prayed hard. *Oh God, I hope Charlie doesn't need me! I'm a good Baptist boy.*

I finished the service, shook the hands of many in my happy flock, and drove back down the hill to our little parsonage.

R-r-ring! I picked up the phone.

"Hi, this is Charlie. We need you tonight!"

Oh, great! What do I do now?

My wheels crunched on the gravel as I pulled up to their trailer and then knocked on the door.

Charlie opened the rickety aluminum door a slit and poked his head around it. "Come on in." He welcomed me into the small space to quite a sight.

His wife's head and hair were flopping all over the place, her eyes unfocused and wild. Her fingers grasped the back of a chair and flipped it over. His wife, Selma, was clearly wigging out ... like she was ... *demon possessed? Is this what it looks like?*

I dug deep into my memory banks for help. I'd heard somewhere in preacher circles that you can just holler and scream at a demon and use the name of Jesus to get rid of it. I thought I'd try it. I puffed out my chest and opened my mouth with all the bravado I could muster.

"GET OUT OF THERE, YOU FILTHY FOUL CREATURE!" I shouted, veins popping on my neck.

She glared back at me.

Then I felt a hand on my shoulder. I thought it was Charlie. He was a great big guy. I turned around, but no one was there. Charlie had a front row seat at the kitchen table.

Then I heard a voice.

Just slow down and be quiet, and I'll show you what to do.

I recognized the voice of the Holy Spirit.

Taking a *deeeeep* breath, I glanced over at the crazy woman again.

The voice said, *This is a demon of lust. Just take authority over it and cast it out.*

Selma was writhing on the bed. Her face contorted like an ugly creature as she glared at me through hateful eyes. I'd never seen anything like it in my life, and I felt the hairs on my back stand on end. Charlie, clasping his big, earth worn hands and slipping a thumb under his patched farmer overalls, paced back and forth in that little place, praying under his breath.

"Come out of her right now in the name of Jesus!" My heart beat wildly, and my brave voice belied my trembling knees.

Selma dropped her head and her body fell limp on the comforter. She drew in a slow breath and raised her head, her pale blue and white eyes shining, and smiled. "So glad to have you here, Pastor!"

Big Charlie stopped and cast a questioning glance at me. I shrugged, relieved that ordeal was finally over. I was ready to leave as soon as possible.

Now when her eyes get red, that's another demon that is about to manifest.

What?

Selma tensed. Her arms jerked and her face contorted again. She sprang off the bed and glared at me hatefully with blood-red eyes, just a few inches from my shocked face.

Oh, no! Here we go again!

This is a spirit of rage, the Holy Spirit whispered.

"Come out, Spirit of Rage, in the name of Jesus!"

Selma became limp again and her eyes white around the pupils as she slumped onto the bed. "That was a mighty good message you preached tonight, Pastor!"

"Ah, yes …"

She cheerfully chatted with us like it was any normal day for several minutes. Then the arteries on her neck popped out, she tensed up again, and her flaming red eyes bulged.

I took a stumbling step back and listened for the Holy Spirit's next instructions. Then, just as if I'd been doing this for years, I took authority over the next so-called demon.

We repeated this over and over again as various spirits manifested and God cast them out using this surprised servant. Thirteen in all! Her poor husband, Charlie, was just as dumbfounded as I. He hadn't known how to handle his wife. Over the past few months, he'd shake his head in wonderment and say, "Brother Frase, she's *crazy!*"

After two hours of wrestling against these invisible forces, Selma's friendly chatter filled the small room for several minutes without any sudden contorting, monstrous facial expressions. I said good-bye and quickly stepped out of the trailer and sped off toward home.

Falling onto the couch next to my sweet wife, Lana, I let out a long sigh. It had been quite an evening of on-the-job training, and I was ready for a good night's sleep.

I never had imagined what was waiting for me as a pastor and leader in the ways of the Lord. I was finding out that I needed plenty of open runways to receive all the dealings of the Holy Spirit. Was I apprehensive? Yes! Was I skeptical? No!

Just cautious and careful, gingerly stepping my way towards more.

Pressing In

The spiritual intensity of what God had done in my heart was drawing me further and forward into understanding the Holy Spirit. I knew what I had experienced was so real and powerful and that it was important to put a biblical basis underneath the Holy Spirit's work in my life.

I had no one to teach or mentor me, and the Holy Spirit said, *I will teach you.* The best teacher in the universe promised to guide me into all truths! Initially, I studied Acts 2, 1 Corinthians 12, 13, and 14. I added John chapters 13 to 15, 1 Corinthians 2, 2 Corinthians 3, Ephesians 4, and 1 Peter 4:10. I was able to trace what many call the baptism of the Holy Spirit through the prophets—Isaiah, Ezekiel, Isaiah, Joel, John the Baptist, Jesus, and Peter.

See Appendix C, "Key Scriptures."

I read as many books as my busy schedule of seminary, a full-time job, pastoring a church, and raising a young family would allow.

And then, Lana and I found out about a rapidly growing Baptist church nearby that was experiencing new spiritual realities.

CHAPTER 8
Baptist Tongues

A little more than a decade after the *Times* picked up the story about a tongue-speaking Episcopal priest in California—which I had read—a spiritual hunger drew me to explore more. While serving at Virginia Hills Baptist Church after receiving the gift of speaking in tongues, and as I mentioned, I dug into more personal Bible study on the gifts of the Holy Spirit.

Beverly Hills Baptist Church

Lana and I learned about a Baptist church where the gifts of the spirit were in operation and the Holy Spirit had liberty in the services (I Corinthians 12). The Beverly Hills Baptist Church in Oak Cliff in South Dallas moved in miraculous ways in the services with dramatic healings and a strong presence of God. We decided to check it out on Wednesday nights.

On that first Wednesday, Lana and I found room on a pew near the back. It was not an impressive-looking church. A plain stage, no balconies, nothing fancy. But throngs of people jampacked the sanctuary, overflowing its outskirts, and reminding me of a spiritual Woodstock. Lana and I looked at one another, wondering what we were in for.

Just like the crowded Jewish synagogue when the paralytic was lowered through the roof and healed. I recalled the comments in the gospel of Mark: "We never saw anything like this!" (Mark 2:12).

A spiritual presence filled the place as people all around us praised the Lord, raising their hands. We were swept away in that first service, and I can't even remember the message. But I do recall how conviction fell on the lost persons wanting to ditch their drugs, who crowded the altar, and that

Lana and I felt the presence of God's glory in the church as Jesus was lifted up. Lana and I had never seen a church service like this before.

I want more of this, I whispered, lifting my hands and heart into a new realm of worship.

Private Meeting with Pastor Conatser

As strange and unconventional as the Beverly Hills Baptist Church was, leaders didn't oust it out of the Southern Baptist Convention, apparently because it was growing like crazy. The church grew from a few hundred to several thousand people in a short time. What could they do? According to the *Abilene Reporter News* on October 20, 1974, the church was too powerful among the 40,000 Southern Baptist churches. A lot of curious Baptists from other churches came to learn what the *charismata* was all about.

The pastor of Beverly Hills, Howard Conatser, claimed he had received the baptism in the Holy Spirit in 1970, and soon after, miraculous healings became a regular part of the service. It was one of those sovereign works of God, and Beverly Hills Baptist was one of the first and most prominent of the Southern Baptist churches in the charismatic movement.

Some believers considered Howard Conatser the "Moses" of the Charismatic Southern Baptists, leading them to the promised land of the Holy Spirit, into a world of real-time healings and miracles. He'd walk out on stage, with his tall, striking white hair and strong features. People regularly piled drugs, needles, and cigarettes around him on the sanctuary stage.

Word of the miracles and healings spread around the world, and people from all over invited him in to preach this charismatic gospel. I knew that what I was experiencing was leading me to travel a path of no return. Not that I wanted to. Just on the fringes of our newly found spiritual walk there was that *more* drawing us deeper and to a higher level. I knew I needed to talk with someone—and why not this pastor?

I nervously dialed Pastor Conatser's number and, surprisingly, got through. "I'm a Baptist pastor and recently baptized in the Holy Spirit with the gift of tongues, pastoring a Baptist church. Can I come see you?"

To my surprise and great fortune, I got a meeting with him. This meeting was a double-edged sword of encouragement and trepidation. The Holy

Spirit had put me under a "gag order" not to tell the congregation about my experience, and I wondered when it would be lifted.

After one of the Wednesday services, Pastor Conatser led me into his office to talk for an hour.

"So … how can I help you?" His kind eyes watched me patiently.

"I'm not sure what to do—I'm a student at Southwestern Seminary. I'm also pastoring Virginia Hills Baptist Church in Athens. This is a difficult situation since our denomination doesn't believe that speaking in tongues is for today."

Pastor Conatser nodded as he listened.

"The Lord told me to 'keep quiet' about it." I clasped my hands and waited for his wise counsel.

"Sooner or later you will talk," he said. "Don't be afraid when that happens. You'll probably get kicked out or be asked to leave."

My mind whirred as I imagined how that might go down. Not a pretty sight.

He smiled, knowingly. Like he'd had this conversation with many others. "Telling the truth about what you've experienced is a decision you'll have to make." He sighed and leaned back in his desk chair. "This is happening everywhere. The Holy Spirit work is happening everywhere, and it does require many decisions. You'll know when the time comes."

I returned to my pastorate with the wisdom of this great man of God. It was clear that I'd soon be coming to a crossroads when I would have to decide how far to go with this new aspect of my quickly developing spiritual life.

The Leadership Meeting Debates

Back at our church, I decided to hold our Sunday evening church training class in debate style to allow the people to sort this issue out for themselves. Quite lively, this debate at least opened some people's eyes to the possibilities of the *more* of the Holy Spirit that I'd found in the scriptures. I stayed neutral in the debate.

One of the ladies in that study came to me after one of the sessions. She looked me right in the eyes, with a thin rivulet of tobacco juice trickling down her chin.

"Do you speak in tongues?" she asked.

I cannot tell you what fright went through my soul as I confessed, "Yes."

"I do, too. And I won't tell anybody."

Whew. Safe to live another Sunday. But it pushed me closer to facing the fact that one day I would need to deal with this.

The Time Had Come: "Tell Them ..."

Even though we conducted our services in the traditional Baptist way, something new and exciting was stirring in our congregation. People from the community were coming to the services and getting saved. We'd pray for people who were sick at the altar, but it was low key and normal looking. The church was filling up. Though 125 attended when I took over the pastorate, we were now at about 200 each Sunday. Our offerings went from $80 a week to more than $1,000. (My salary was $75 per week.) We had to add on new rooms in the height of spiritual revival.

I grew bolder and began to teach through the book of Acts on Sunday mornings, incorporating some of the things I'd learned in my private study. One Sunday, I opened my Bible to Acts 2:1–4 and read:

> When the Day of Pentecost had fully come, they were all with one accord in one place. And suddenly there came a sound from heaven, as of a rushing mighty wind, and it filled the whole house where they were sitting. Then there appeared to them divided tongues, as of fire, and one sat upon each of them. And they were all filled with the Holy Spirit and began to speak with other tongues, as the Spirit gave them utterance.

When I finished, the Holy Spirit whispered, *Tell them.*

Tell them what?

Tell them that you've had this same experience.

I thought, *Oh, no. Is this the moment Pastor Conatser said would come?* This would be my spiritual Rubicon. There comes a time in all of our lives when we must move on and never turn back—in the nature of life and in our spiritual walk.

I took a deep breath, looked out to the people I'd grown to love and care for in this little country church on the hill, then turned away and stalled, ready to argue with God. *If they knew that I, too, spoke in tongues, that will be the end of my pastorate here!* The bylaws stated that if the church ever ceased to become Southern Baptist in nature, we'd lose the building. And I'd surely be kicked out.

My mouth opened before I could stop it. "I have been baptized in the Holy Spirit, and I speak in a special language, the gift of tongues, like the Bible talks about … And it is *wun-der-ful …*"

In every life there are decision moments when we have to stand for biblical truth and experience, the times when we declare what God has done, what the Holy Spirit is doing, no matter what family, friends, or foes might say or do. Sometimes the Holy Spirit will speak for us to do so. Other times we just come to the moment to do so. Well, I truly felt that the church received my surprise announcement. Little did I know!

Little did I know that the preacher was being roasted over the dinner table that day, and the opposing forces began the typical process of ousting us. It would be just a couple of weeks when it all would come to a head.

CHAPTER 9
Booted Out!

Surprisingly, no one stood up and yelled at me or shook fists. No riot broke out in the pews; no ladies threw their hats at me.

In fact, a few people smiled.

Yeah, God, we pulled it off!

I shook hands and chatted with people as they filed out the door.

More closet Charismatics came to our services. And those more vocal. And this threatened the old guard. They didn't want tongue-talkers in their space. What I didn't realize is that they were gathering forces behind the scenes to kick Lana and me out.

One afternoon, I came home from seminary to the parsonage. Lana was at the door, crying.

"What's the matter?"

"The deacons have called a meeting."

"That's okay," I said.

"No, it isn't. People have been calling me all afternoon. The deacons are calling a special meeting, and it doesn't look good …"

The Meeting

Lana and I nervously walked through the door of a boardroom with about five pairs of eyes staring up at us. Only 31 years old, I was almost too young and naive to fear about our future or to realize the nuances of a church power struggle.

The area minister opened the meeting for discussion. We liked him a lot.

Don, a deacon, blurted, "The church has got to stop going the way it is going."

"Yes, if we don't stop this doctrinal runaway train," another red-faced member said, "our mother church will take this church away from us, according to the bylaws."

The area minister surveyed the tense room with kindness deepening his wrinkled face. "Anything Brother Frase is doing that is not biblical?"

Silence. Then noises, like fingers tapping on the conference table, the buzz of a fan, a throat clearing filled in the awkward silence. A long, awkward pause filled the room as questioning eyes darted back and forth.

Finally, one flustered deacon spoke. "It may be biblical, but it's not *Baptist!*"

They argued on and on. Things had blown way out of our control.

One member stood and opened his wallet as he asked, "How much money will it take you to leave?"

Another stood and pulled out his wallet and repeated the offer.

I couldn't believe these brothers were trying to buy us off! Well, the wise mediator called the meeting.

We walked out of the room into the dark night, confused and wondering, *What's next?*

Next Steps

Lana went to the house while I left in another direction to clear my mind. I walked down the country road with the moon shining through the pine trees and contemplated what had just happened. *This is a spiritual crossroad.* An important one. One that would require a decision that would change the trajectory of our lives.

What do I do, Lord? Should I go or stay?

Though the night was not cold, I shivered. Fear of the unknown gripped me. Of losing my dear Baptist friends. Of losing my church after years of education. And, I'd lose the small amount they gave to help support my family.

Is going in another direction away from our church here worth being put on a trash heap of ridicule and scorn? Where will we go? How will we start over? Where would we live? It's not like we have six months to prepare.

The board met on a Thursday night, and I was thinking of resigning on Sunday. Quitting seemed like a foolish decision. I wondered if there was any way to stay and work it out. *Is it really over?*

I thought about my experiences in Corban, Kentucky, at the teen revival, the late night discussion with my fellow Baptist seminary student Dave, and the year of studying the scriptures on my own. As I considered our leadership meeting debates and my own experiences with a new and exciting filling of the Holy Spirit with evidence of speaking in tongues, I couldn't imagine how I could continue to preach and leave out texts in the scriptures that seemed so important. And we had seen the gifts in operation at the Beverly Hills Baptist church—up close and personal.

As I looked up at the moon again, this time a beacon in the shadows, I saw a fork in the road in my journey. One path led me down a predictable way of success in the Baptist church, where I buddied up to these deacons and elders, following the dictates of my seminary teaching—and kept a lid on the experiences of the Holy Spirit now dropping onto the expanding runways of my heart. It was a wide path of pleasing others.

The other runway would take us to unfamiliar places and could open new areas of our hearts to new venues of ministry. And lead down a more narrow, mysterious winding path. One where I was, oddly enough, propelled by surrender. Surrender to the move and workings of the Holy Spirit. Surrender from the things *I wanted*—with all my pride and ego—to the things God had for me. Whatever they were. Surrender to a voice that said, "I will teach you how …"

I realized that night that there was no turning back, but also that there would be a cost to moving forward—I couldn't recant. How could I turn my back on the third member of the Trinity and His gifts and workings and dealings with me? How could I follow man and not what I felt in my heart God was showing me?

During that week, the pastor of the Baptist church downtown that we reported to strongly suggested we leave town.

These considerations plagued my mind and kept me tossing and turning in bed at night. I needed to make the decision right away. Here I was, not even graduated from seminary, and the church board wanted to boot me out of my first church!

While I thought about these things, I found out later, the congregation was already getting wind of the meeting. Several busied themselves gleefully spreading the fire.

DIME for a PHONE CALL

Russ and Lana told about a spat early in their marriage that left Lana looking for a phone booth in the middle of the rolling hills countryside.

Lana said, "We'd been booted out of the church and the parsonage. An Assembly of God couple opened up their beautiful home in the country for us for a couple of years. This was when we were on the college campus. Russ was so wrapped up in ministry. And when he was home, he worked. And me with two little kids! I finally got fed up!"

With a big grin Russ leaned back in his chair and said "Gotta call her sister and mama!"

Ignoring him, Lana narrowed her eyes and continued. "There was always somebody who needed that Yankee boy of mine in the middle of the night and he would go."

"Yeah, we had some kind of a heated, intense argument ..." Russ said.

"Beeeeecause, you were always busy helping that person, that person ..." Then she added, "I'm a firm believer in murder or divorce!"

"Lana took the stroller and went out the door—in the middle of the country! She had to go a long way down a dirt road to find a phone booth. She's gotta call *Mama* ..."

Lana shot back, "And Mama would have come and gotten me, too."

Explaining it, he said, "The night we got married, her daddy gave her a dime and said, 'If you need me, call me.' ... I guess she was cashing in that dime."

Guests soon discover how much the Frase couple love to spar with one another, even 50 years later.

Our Decision

Lana and I talked it over and we agreed—we needed to leave Virginia Hills Baptist Church. I wrote a letter of resignation effective next Sunday.

I knew that in order to embrace the future we had to release the past. So where would we go from there? We were uncertain, and Lana was still stunned from the response. Isn't it amazing that when we were halfway to change we were both afraid of going forward and backward. Only the Holy Spirit can sort that out!

The sun rose on a clear, crisp September day as Lana dressed Paula, and we prepared to close a door in that little farm congregation, my first church, and the place God had taught us so much.

I stood at the pulpit with bittersweet emotions, surveyed the people I'd grown to love, and read my resignation. I concluded, "God has called me to Athens, so we won't be leaving this town. We will be starting a new work uptown somewhere." I stepped down, took Lana by the hand and walked out the door.

The worship leader, who had

become a good friend, followed us out onto the front steps, his eyes big and questioning. "What the *hell* is going on here?"

CHAPTER 10

Finding New Life
at New Life Church

Following that Sunday of departure in September 1975, we discovered a building we could rent on the campus of the Henderson County community college. We cleaned out the meeting area on a Saturday night so we could begin services Sunday morning.

The first Sunday service of New Life Church, 99 people worshipped with us. Many were from Virginia Hills Church. When they found out we were going to be a charismatic church, they didn't come back, thinning our membership to 17.

We stayed in north Athens in the junior college building for six months. The church grew to 50, and I graduated from seminary that December with a Master of Divinity.

Then, around March 1976, God moved us to another building, ironically right across from the Baptist church that had planted the church that had kicked us out!

One morning, during the offering time, the Lord gave me a vision of a piece of land we were going to build on and that somebody would give it to us.

Not long after that, a man who listened to me preach on the radio called one day. He told me he had a piece of land he'd like to consider giving, and would I come see him?

With my hands sweating, I knocked on his door.

"So, *that's* what you look like!" he exclaimed, laughing, as he looked at my long dark hair.

We talked about the land, and he decided to give me his choice three

Horses at the Starting Gate

By Russ Frase

Interestingly, my twin brother, Roy, who ignored our dad's preaching right along with me as we played practical tricks on the adults, got saved and filled with the Holy Spirit right about the same time as me across the continent. I didn't find out till later. Now we serve together in ministry at times. He's a great friend who celebrated his 50th wedding anniversary with Gale within months of Lana and me in 2018, and we like to kid each other a lot.

When I visit Roy in upstate New York, we like to go to the famous horse raceway in Saratoga Springs, an impressive 350-acre racetrack that caters to thoroughbred horse racing surrounded by 30,000 people yelling in the stands.

I love watching the horses run. They are magnificent creatures of massive flesh and muscle that hurl themselves around the final stretch to the finish line.

Watching them enter their assigned starting gate is enlightening. Some move in with no difficulty, while others struggle. Others enter hesitantly, balking or backing away, and their trainers have to prod, shove, and even force them into their starting stalls. Their owners know that if their horse does not enter the gate, it will not be allowed to start the race.

Many Christians approach the starting gate in the work of the Holy Spirit the same way. Some believers enter right into the flow of the Holy Spirit while others need a gentle,

continued...

acres in uptown Athens. We called it "High Cotton" because that's where the rich people lived.

Then a Methodist lady who owned two acres behind that land sold her land to us. God was moving and providing for our growing congregation.

Problems in Building

And so we broke ground on our first building. No church building program is without its difficulties. Ours was no exception. After we'd trenched out the foundation structure, we needed a plumber. The one we'd scheduled backed out on us.

A husband of one of the women in our church was a plumber—but with a problem. Yes, I literally got him out of a bar (10 sheets to the wind!) to come and set the plumbing to be ready for when men showed up the next day to pour the foundation.

"How could you *do* such a thing?" my leaders asked.

But I determined we'd get 'er done! In the dark, I rustled up 15 members and directed them to shine their lights on my "buddy plumber" as he worked.

And, by Jove, around 10:30 p.m., it was done.

The following days, the walls went up, the rafters were fitted into place, and the plywood roof nailed down. At the time, I substitute taught in the high school. One day when I was teaching, administrators called me out of my class to the phone.

This must be serious.

"Russ! Russ!" Lana's voice wavered on the other end.

"What's the matter?"

"The building fell down!"

"What?"

"The building blew down! The wind came and blew the framed walls down, and the rafters and everything are laying on the ground!"

encouraging prod to get into position. Unfortunately a few balk and back away from cooperating with the Holy Spirit and never start the race. They feel that the baptism of the Holy Spirit and all the gifts of the Holy Spirit that the Bible mentions are not for them. Therefore, they never enter the race nor get to experience all the greater spiritual victories in the backstretch because they did not receive the fullness of the Holy Spirit.

It is the great desire of the heavenly Father, who gave us the promise of the Holy Spirit, that we all enter freely and fully into the Holy Spirit's starting gate to run the race He's destined for us.

No matter what kind of horse you may be, no matter how hesitant you are in exploring and embracing the Holy Spirit in its fullness in your life, it is my desire as you read this book that you will discover ways to run and finish the race God offers to every believer.

"That's what you get for using a drunk plumber! God cursed it," someone told us later. (I'll ask God when I get to heaven what happened.)

Our Church: Not Much to Look At

That first church we built was plain looking—an uncomfortable 3200-square-foot building that we didn't even have sense to put windows in. We didn't have enough money for a paved parking lot—it was red dirt. If you didn't make it to the service in time to park there, you parked out on the field. And if it was raining—and it rained a lot in our little town in Texas—cars spun out in the mud. Women's shoes got stuck, too. We ruined a lot of shoes! It was embarrassing. I told the ladies, "We'll pay for your shoes!" I mean, it was a nightmare.

The back door was just a back door, no awning or drive-through. You just opened the door, and you were walking on the concrete floor sanctuary, trailing in red dirt and all. And the chairs were those cheap metal, folding kind. Very primitive. And when I was preaching, my head practically hit the ceiling.

But the Spirit of God moved in a powerful way in our congregation. I learned quickly that everything the Holy Spirit ministered to me, I was to minister to others. As I studied about the spiritual gifts and about the great evangelists, such as George Whitefield, John and Charles Wesley, I learned how people would fall out of their seats overcome by the power of God, staggering around supposedly drunk, not on wine but drunk on the Holy Spirit. Week after week, God healed people in our church in miraculous ways, and the gifts of the Spirit manifested in ways that continually amazed us. We were all learning together.

So people didn't mind what the building looked like or how uncomfortable it was. They were eager to see what God would do next. Many were getting filled in deeper ways with the Holy Spirit, even without others laying hands on them. We prayed for the sick all the time. Lana would not miss our church services for anything. She loved the people and the excitement the Holy Spirit was generating in our little body of believers.

Several people joined the church from that part of town and helped us continue to grow and build a church where the Holy Spirit was free to move as He spilled his gifts out all over us. Novices to the experiences and manifestations of the Holy Spirit, we didn't need to be deprogrammed from false, traditional, and others' teachings. We simply lived out the book of Acts for the next 10 years the way we saw it in the Scriptures, eager to learn new things from the Holy Spirit each day.

CHAPTER 11
Close Calls

One of the greatest salvation stories I hold dear to my heart is that of Bill. A recluse way back in the woods, he left people alone and they left him alone. People often saw him sitting on the guardrails on the nearby highway reading the newspaper. We'd heard he collected the daily news and they were stacked in his two-room log cabin to the ceiling. And that he covered himself at night with the newspapers for warmth.

Everyone left him alone, except for "Preacher Frase."

"Lana, let's go see Bill."

She'd gotten used to my strange ways and said okay.

We drove the winding road through the tall pine trees for miles to his cabin and parked.

Knock. Knock.

He opened the door and peered out, his scraggly beard looking like he'd stuck it on his face with super glue. The hair that circled his bald spot stuck out unapologetically. A smell *whooshed* through the doorway as he opened the door all the way. We walked in like we owned the place, noting that, indeed, stacks of newspapers were the decor of his homestead.

"Hi, I'm Pastor Frase." I stuck out my hand, smiling brightly.

He shook it hesitantly.

"And I'm Lana." My beautiful wife graciously kicked away some papers to move further into the room beside me.

We spent about 15 minutes of mostly silence with him. But I also shared about Jesus, who loved him, died for his sins on a cross but had risen again. Standing in an awkward circle, he watched me a bit skeptically. A warm love and compassion filled my heart for Bill. Faith welled up inside. *Our prayers and the Holy Spirit will bring him to salvation one day.*

Three years later, a team of paramedics carted Bill off to a hospital in Tyler. He was dying.

"Could you please go and see Bill?" pleaded one of his few friends.

As I entered his hospital room, I saw the shadow of a man with tubes coming out of every part of his body. His eyes were closed. As the sounds of the machines beeped and gurgled I thought, *He's barely conscious. Am I too late?*

Then the Holy Spirit told me the words I should say to him, words that would penetrate that fog of semi-consciousness and reach him. God released the "gift of faith" to believe for him to be saved (1 Corinthians 12:9). Though a young pastor, I felt this gift well up inside me. I prayed under my breath for Bill.

"Bill, it's Pastor Frase. I want to share with you how you can have all your sins forgiven, accept Jesus, and go to heaven."

He didn't move.

"They tell me you're dying ... so I'm going to share the gospel with you."

A machine beeped.

I gently took his hand in mine. Lying alone and helpless and hopeless on that hospital bed, he seemed so unready to enter eternity. "When you hear and understand what I am saying, squeeze my hand. I know you can't talk, but the Bible says in Romans 10:9, 'If you confess with your mouth the Lord Jesus and believe in your heart that God raised Him from the dead, you will be saved. For with the heart a person believes unto righteousness, and with the mouth confession is made into salvation.'

"I know you can't talk, Bill, but squeeze my hand if you believe in your heart and mind what I am saying."

He squeezed.

I shared more.

He squeezed again, without opening his eyes.

Tears fell down my cheeks as I continued to talk and he continued to squeeze my hand.

Then I noticed tears streaming from his closed eyes.

I've never witnessed anything so beautiful as Bill accepting Jesus and eternal life. There he was, this man nobody wanted anything to do with. He was the least, the lost, the left out, and the last—except for the saving grace of Jesus.

No matter where we are, God has our number and location and will send someone to bring us the good news.

Bill died that day. Though his life on earth ended, he slipped into eternity to enjoy a life he never had here. A life with Jesus.

And I'll bet this redeemed recluse is waiting in glory for me, to thank me, a big smile on his face, and probably with a newspaper in his hands.

Saved on His Deathbed

"Please, please, have more roast beef," Bertha said, passing a large platter to me, grinning. On the table before Lana, Paula, Rusty, and me she'd placed an incredible spread of different kinds of meat, potatoes, poke salad, steaming hot buttered rolls, and three kinds of mouth-watering pies—including banana cream, one of my favorites. She'd invited our family for Sunday dinner after my preaching at New Life, like many times before, and had gotten up at 5 a.m. to cook.

Her husband, Tommy, cut a big chunk of meat and stuffed it in his mouth. A satisfied smile spread across his face as he sank deeper into his chair. He barely tolerated that we came with the meal—he'd been hurt by many preachers and tried to avoid us. (Old-fashioned and a bit set in his ways, Tommy stashed his money in a sock in the wall, I discovered.)

An incredible lady and a great hostess, Bertha also had an ulterior motive for inviting us on Sunday afternoons. As a lady of faith, she wanted us to spend time with her husband and her brood of seven or eight sons and daughters and the grandkids that came by on Sunday afternoons from

Top Ten Ways to Hear the Voice of God

Through:

1. The Word of God
2. Our thought structures
3. Meditation on God's truths
4. Dreams and visions
5. An audible voice
6. Good counsel of others
7. Impressions, inner promptings, and holy hunches
8. Mental snapshots
9. Conversation: asking God questions and listening to answers from Him
10. The Spirit man, by the Holy Spirit

—From the June 2010 Joshua Nations Newsletter

Dallas. Their boozing and drugging ways broke her heart, but with determination, she connected us to them, hoping somehow Lana and I'd minister to them and influence them.

We ate first with Tommy and Bertha right after church. Then, like a weekly family reunion, the rest would pound on the door and tumble into the living room around 2:00 p.m.—10 to 15 of them, boisterous, some with tattoos and straggly hair, kids wrestling—for the second round of the feast. Country at heart, they enjoyed escaping the big city and hanging out with family on the acreage in the well-worn house with rickety cupboard shelves without doors, undeterred by the sound of wind shaking the glass windows.

Bertha's kids liked me because I showed up frequently to help their parents, like the time I plowed and planted Bertha's garden with her. Despite their wild ways, I grew fond of the family, and they appreciated my unconditional acceptance of them. They considered me the friend they could call in need: one phoned late one night from the district attorney's office high on either alcohol or drugs for my help. (After we moved to Arvada, Colorado, two grandsons committed suicide, and I flew back to Texas to grieve with the family and conduct their funerals.)

We knew Bertha from our Virginia Hills church days, and she followed us to New Life. The Frase family stayed involved in their lives. As I stood on the porch one sunny day, Tommy opened the door and called me by my first name—the first time he'd ever done that. The Holy Spirit whispered to my heart, *You got him!* assuring me that Tommy would accept Him one day.

One Wednesday in January, Bertha called the church and told staff that Tommy was in bad shape and probably wouldn't live long. Folks in the church anointed me, and I drove to their house—that familiar house usually filled with savory dinner smells. With fear in her eyes, Bertha ushered me into their bedroom where a small number of the family solemnly stood, including Rita, a daughter who also knew the Lord.

Tommy's gray and wrinkled face turned up and he looked at me. He tried to say something, but coughed and wheezed and couldn't get a word out.

I stood by his bed, tears in my eyes, thinking of the 75 times (no exaggeration) I'd visited him in the course of five or six years. I'd shared the gospel on occasion, or shared what God was doing in our lives. Not once did he ever show an interest in spiritual things.

Why is this time any different?

But as I looked at him, I wondered how long he'd be gasping for breath on this earth. Didn't look like long. I could tell by the fear in his wife's eyes that she was afraid of his eternal destination.

I asked him if we could pray, and he nodded. I took his hand, and an electrical power shot through my hand and into him and his body! And he responded. That night Tommy gave his life to Christ, with Bertha and Rita standing nearby, crying with tears of gratitude.

He died 36 hours later.

I conducted Tommy's funeral, grieving for the family's loss and loving them through it. Bertha continued to invite our family for dinner in their home.

One of the deacons, skilled in cabinetry, gave Bertha a bid to fix and enclose the cabinets in her kitchen. She accepted it and he did the work. One day, Bertha called me quite upset. Our deacon had upped the price to double the original. That made me furious—especially since we'd spent so much time developing a friendship with the family.

I called the deacon and asked, "What's going on?"

"Turns out there was more work than I'd originally thought."

"No way!" The veins popped out on my neck. "You charge that sweet widow lady what you told her it would cost!"

Bertha invited her gang to Easter Sunday service a few months later. "I'm not sure if they'll come," she told me wistfully.

But her kids, whom I'd grown to know and love despite all their dysfunctions, decided that, in honor of their dad, they'd attend this Resurrection Sunday service I'd preach.

After the message, the Lord whispered to me how He wanted me to give an altar call. I closed my eyes and said the words that came. As I opened my eyes, I saw almost every one of Bertha's family walking up to the altar sifted in between others coming, and tearfully surrendering their lives to Christ.

Flashes of the many times I'd talked to them on those Sunday afternoons, the trouble they'd get into and out of, the regular moments of life we'd lived together, and the funeral of their dad and the grief we'd all shared went through my mind as I saw the precious children and grandchildren of Bertha's kneeling at the altar as new creations in Christ. I thought of how God honored a sweet widow's heart cry as she sowed into their lives and the lives of my family year after year. He honored His principle of sowing and reaping: Bertha's faithfulness of sowing in ours and others' lives God returned with the salvation of her family.

This was the first time I had the privilege of being so hands-on with a family like this, and it touched my soul to stand at the altar and watch them publicly exchange their old lives for new ones.

Many of the brood began going to church and living for the Lord.

All of our lives dramatically changed during that 12 years of doing life together.

CHAPTER 12
Dramatic Transformations

As I stood at the front of my small congregation at our service in the new church building we'd proudly built in the *high cotton* neighborhood of Athens, I glanced at two of our elders to the left, standing in front of metal chairs. The service had started half an hour ago, and they were lost in some other place, big smiles on their faces. Sweet music and a warm presence swirled all around us and filled us, overflowing. It was tangible, thick. Some of the faces of the people bore tears, some eyes lifted to heaven, others stood in the aisle, hands uplifted.

This has nothing to do with me or what I just said. My eyes were wide as I took in the scene.

The presence of the Holy Spirit was particularly strong.

An unshaven man dressed in worn jeans and a faded shirt staggered up the aisle toward me, trying to miss the worshippers in his path, and fell down at the altar.

Tommy! I recognized our town drunk. Tommy was a fixture in our town, hanging out in front of shops and staggering down the sidewalks and streets. He was a good-natured drunk—not mean or abusive to his family. But addiction wrapped its evil claws around him and held him in its vile grip, filling him with shame and hopelessness.

Tears streamed down Tommy's face as he lifted it from the floor and held up his hands. I could hear him only because he was so close.

"God, I am so sorry! I need you!"

Others came down the aisle and fell to the floor. Some accepted Jesus into their hearts for the first time. Many begged for change in their lives.

The Three-line Newspaper Ad that Changed a Life

"Woman, don't ever say that to me again!" His red eyes bore into his wife's scared ones as he pressed the sharp knife to her throat.

This is the last time you are doing this to me. She clenched her teeth, determined to take their two kids and leave.

When she divorced her husband, her church rejected her and the people shunned them.

Lonely and hurting, she picked up the newspaper and a three-line ad, hidden in an obscure part of the paper caught her eye, advertising a new church in town. New Life Church, meeting in a civic building downtown.

"Let's go visit this church I've read about," she told the kids.

When they walked into the church's meeting room one Sunday night, people overwhelmed them with their smiles, hugs, and welcoming words.

"I could play the piano for you," she told Pastor Frase.

Later he found out she worked as Chief Financial Officer for one of the businesses in Athens.

"Would you like to be our church treasurer?"

She accepted, and became a great help to Pastor Frase and to the church. She gratefully remembered the three-line ad that changed her life.

Tears sprang into my eyes as I realized it didn't matter if they were up at the front or in their seats, or at the back of the room. God was doing something here.

Sleeping Disease

There's somebody who's not here, but should be here. I recognized the Holy Spirit's voice, and knew He wanted me to faithfully repeat it out loud to the people.

"Let's pray for these people right now."

We prayed. We continued to worship. More people moved out of their seats.

Fifteen minutes later, two ladies with two kids I've never seen before sank into four metal chairs in the back.

These are the people.

One lady sobbed, eyes lowered.

What's going on? How can I help? But I sensed I was not supposed to do anything. I didn't notice when she slipped into the aisle. She stood before me among the others who were crying and praying at the front, and she raised her tearful eyes to me.

"How can I help you?" I asked.

"I have a sleeping disease. I sleep day and night. I can't be a mother to my kids, a wife to my husband."

She told me her name was Beverly. "And I was just healed."

"How do you know?"

"I just feel it. I was healed."

"Are you on medicine?"

"Yes, I have been on it for years."

"Okay, don't throw away your medicine. Go back to the doctor."

A couple of weeks later in the church hallway, Beverly tapped me on the back, eager to share. "I've just had the most amazing week. I went home after church that night, slept well, got up and cleaned my house the next day. And, with more energy than ever, I helped the kids the day after that. Do you know how long it's been?"

"Congratula—"

"And that's not all! I went back to the doctor. He ran some tests. He said he doesn't know how it happened, but I am completely healed of the disease."

I opened my mouth to speak.

"I've never been to a church like this before, nor seen anything like it in my life!" She danced away toward the door, lightly taking a hand of each kid in hers.

I learned there are things that only the Holy Spirit can do and we must not interfere with His operation. He led Beverly to get ready and go to New Life Church. He healed her of the disease without anyone laying hands on her, without anointing her with oil, without everyone praying for her.

I was learning how to be sensitive to what the Lord tells us, especially in worship. I saw Him bring people in, save them, move them to come to the altar without an altar call.

I had no idea Beverly's nonstop sleeping disease was only one small part of her problems. But soon, she invited me to glimpse into her strange world.

On the Other Side of the Tracks

Beverly's husband was a biker with The Bad Choppers out of Corpus Christi. He had come to Athens to hide because some guys were after him. For what, who knew?

One Friday night about three weeks after Beverly was healed, she called me, hysterical. "Chase is going to kill me! He's going to kill me!"

"Beverly, where are you?"

She gave me her home address.

I was scared, too, but knew I had to do something. "I'll be back," I called out to Lana as I grabbed my coat and slammed the door, without even thinking maybe I should bring someone along with me just in case.

I revved up my puke green Maverick (which would stall at the most inconvenient times), my white hands clenching the steering wheel, drove across town past the railroad tracks, and turned into a messed-up looking neighborhood.

Peering through the eerie dusk, the worn and missing address numbers made it difficult to find Beverly's house. I made out the numbers on a house in bad need of repair. A broken-down car with a missing fender sat in the driveway. The front yard was a junkyard of empty cans and bottles and unwanted boards. *I wonder if they are filled with rusty nails.*

I quickly turned off the engine and slid out of the seat, surveying the landscape with wide eyes, ready for any lurking danger.

Pi-ang! As I picked my way across the yard, the clanking can at my feet caused me to jump, and I walked rapidly up to the front door, feigning courage.

I hadn't noticed, but the torn screen door stood ajar, and a hulking, dark-haired man with huge tattooed biceps took a step toward me out of the shadow. He stepped onto the porch and glared at me.

I froze.

No, he was looking past me with glazed eyes, and a sickening smell wafted out from the house. His hair was matted with blood that traveled down his face in rivulets. I'd obviously missed a pretty nasty fight.

Lord, what do I do?

Just lay your hands on him and tell the demon spirit to come out of him.

I lifted my trembling hand, wondering where Beverly was. But I knew the Lord wanted me to deal with this here and now.

This guy could break me in two.

"In the name of Jesus, you foul spirit—come out of him!"

His eyes cleared and his shoulders relaxed, and he looked at me quizzically, then smiled. What a sight! A big tattooed dude with bloodied matted hair, smiling at me. I heard tiny feet shuffle a few feet ahead in the house and noticed young kids peering around Beverly's legs in the living room as she watched.

"Won't you come in?" She looked back and forth from her husband to me. My hands still trembling as I heard the *thunk! thunk!* of my heart in my ears, I followed them to their torn and worn-out brown couch.

I told him about God's forgiveness through Jesus Christ His Son, who hung on a cross to die for him—no matter what he'd done. He shocked me by nodding, yes, he'd like to receive this Jesus into his heart. It emboldened me.

"Chase, I want you to come to church on Sunday morning."

"Oh, preacher, they won't accept me there."

"Yes ... I want you to come."

Two days later before our church service, I thought of Chase. I wondered if he'd actually come. Did he even get saved?

Sure enough, he showed up at the back of the church with Beverly and his kids in tow in the middle of my message. He clunked down the aisle in his workers' boots, complete with biker T-shirt, bulging muscles, and chains clanking against the metal chairs. His family followed close behind.

A big smile filled my face. *I wonder what they'll think. I wonder what they'll do.* As I surveyed my flock, I saw accepting smiles and approving looks.

The noisy entourage made it to the front row, and they sat right in front of me, eight pairs of eyes waiting.

I turned a page, took a breath, and finished my message.

Chase, Beverly, and the family mysteriously left town not long after that. I found out later in a strange coincidental meeting what had happened. Chase apparently witnessed a murder and fled for his life with his family.

I ran into them again a few years later in a most surprising circumstance.

CHAPTER 13
Miracles

Oftentimes miracles don't happen because we are begging God to do them. They usually don't happen in the way we want, think, or expect. Sometimes they occur in an extraordinary manner. But usually because we are obedient to the last thing He tells us to do.

The first century church was told to go and tarry in Jerusalem and wait for the power to settle on them—a power they would need in order to expand the church (Acts 1:4–8). One of those powers I discovered is the power of miraculous healing.

As we traveled this journey of discovery—how to model the first century Christians—I prayed, *Holy Spirit, manifest Yourself as You desire. Whatever You want, I want. Whatever giftings You want to use today and in our midst, use them. Help me be sensitive and in Your will.* If the Holy Spirit did nothing, that was fine with me, but it was rare that He didn't.

Paul also instructs in 1 Corinthians 14:26–33 and 40 for all things, including the function of the gifts of the Spirit to be done decently and in order. "For God is not the author of confusion but of peace" (33).

And, at New Life church, they were. Every now and then we'd get something in the flesh. The motive of the heart of the one ministering is so key. We knew nothing, but our hearts were pure.

The Miraculous Healing the Townspeople Noticed

Our town newspaper was the *kahuna* of communications, and a well-known figure in our community, Laverne, edited the paper. Around 1976, a terrible auto accident damaged her spine so badly that neurosurgeons told her she'd never walk again. Undeterred, this editor on the hunt for information

The Miraculous Healing from a Child's Point of View

Told by Penny Ikner
RMBI graduate, Joshua Nations Rep and Director of Nursing of a Skilled Nursing Facility

It's So Simple

Shortly after my family started attending New Life Church, I was saved at Vacation Bible School at the age of 7. About 35 of us came to VBS in the evenings and learned Bible stories. On the last night, Pastor Russ asked who would like to follow him into a room and accept Jesus into their hearts. I noticed a nice lady at the meetings always gave out lollipops, so when he asked that, I looked at her candy longingly and thought I might get one if I joined the kids.

Though my motives were wrong, I watched this tall, kind pastor kneel on the floor in front of our little group of five. He invited us to kneel, too. But, being a contrary person even at that age, I wondered, *Why are we on our knees?*

As though he read my mind, he looked gently into each of our eyes with love and tears in his and said, "We are getting on our knees at the feet of Jesus to give our lives to Him." He explained the gospel in such simple terms, all my questions disappeared.

It's so easy! Why didn't I do that sooner?

When I left the room, I got the lollipop, too.

The Miracle after 24/7 Prayer!

A few years later on Palm Sunday,

continued...

traveled to Houston, San Francisco, and other cities for a year and met with nine different neurosurgeons seeking answers. She had surgery that cut nerves in the legs to relieve pain, and they were now completely atrophied and limp. It was physically impossible for her to ever walk on them again.

In 1977, about a year after we moved into our church building, ironically the head deacon from the Baptist church that oversaw the first church I pastored and that booted us out, rolled Laverne into our little service on a hospital bed to the back of the church. She'd heard about miracles in our church and decided her only chance was to seek healing at New Life.

When I saw the deacon wheel her in, I froze. *Oh, God, You've got to do something here. Could You please extend the worship? I have no idea what to do.*

God was about to expand the runways of my heart in a new way—whether I gave Him permission or not. There are times in the life of the Spirit that overwhelming challenges come—an opportunity to do a kingdom work, like heal the sick. I sensed the Holy Spirit tell me, *Get all of the men. Line them up behind her, hold hands forming a chain. I'll heal her.*

I took a deep breath. "Could all the men line up behind Laverne and form a chain around her?" I heard the sound of many feet shuffling on the concrete floor as they moved into place. As I grasped the hand of the man right behind me, I felt the surge of healing power of God flow through me and to this lady.

Tell her to walk.

I froze. *What if she doesn't? Here's the head deacon of that church! I will look like a fool all over town! Boy, they are going to laugh at us …*

Fear paralyzed me. So I didn't tell her—easier that way. And she didn't get up.

Guilt, shame, failure hung around my neck like a heavy chain that afternoon. As I reviewed the scene over and over in my mind that week, the week leading up to the glorious Resurrection Sunday, discouragement and depression filled my heart. I berated myself for failing to obey the Holy Spirit. I'd blown it. I'd

with my mother sitting next to me in church, I turned around and noticed a strange sight: a bed on rollers in the back with a large lady lying on it. *Why would someone come to church in a bed?*

The people in our church loved to pray—they did it all the time—and sometime during or after the service, we prayed for this lady. And then the man who brought her wheeled her away. This lady wasn't a member of our church, but rather someone in need in our community. Pastor Russ asked people to go to the hospital where doctors and nurses cared for her in groups of two around the clock during the next week and pray for her. My mom volunteered. No one could go with her so one day that week she drove to the hospital by herself in a torrential rainstorm and prayed for the lady in her room from 2:00 a.m. till 6:00 a.m.

The next Sunday—Easter Sunday—people crowded into our church sanctuary. The rest of my family wasn't with us, but Mom and I had gotten there early enough to grab seats in the middle. Mom sat next to the middle aisle and I was next to her.

I turned around and saw the same lady in her bed in the back of the church. She had come back!

A lady at the front had the most beautiful, long brown hair. When she opened her mouth to sing, she sounded like an angel straight from heaven. People all around me were crying and it felt as if the room were flooded with something very warm and wonderful.

Suddenly, while the lady was still singing, I saw Pastor Russ walking toward us down the aisle with a couple

continued…

of men behind him. He was intently looking at something at the back of the church, set on getting to it.

Then I heard a sound next to me and *there was the lady I'd seen on the bed—walking down the aisle toward Pastor Russ—just a few feet from me!*

I tugged on Mom's arm. "She's in her nightgown!"

The lady with the beautiful hair stopped singing.

Mom's eyes grew big as she watched the lady in her PJs walk proudly forward. "We are watching a miracle!" she whispered loudly.

Complete silence filled the sanctuary as people held their breath, eyes on the center aisle, taking in what had just happened. Then I heard gasps all around me.

Pastor Russ, eyes filled with tears, met her halfway and the sound of his voice exploding with joy as he praised God and spoke in a language I didn't know. Then a rolling thunder, a roaring of praise erupted throughout the church!

In that moment, something penetrated my heart and took me to a whole different place. The lady couldn't get out of her bed before the service. Then she walked down the aisle!

I wonder how many people in church that morning had gone to that hospital room to pray for her the previous week. I also can't help but wonder who else was touched in a supernatural way that Easter morning.

They took the lady back to the hospital—as my mom recalls, doctors had given her only a window of three hours to leave and attend church before her regularly scheduled pain

continued...

failed the test, and a lady missed her healing.

To make matters worse, I learned that week who she was and that *everybody* knew her. No telling what people in the community were saying about their newspaper editor and the failed healing. I agonized as the enemy played his best cards against me.

Next Sunday, Easter, people from the community packed our church standing room only. The door opened and in came that hospital bed again with Laverne on top, pushed by the Baptist deacon.

My mind churned with mixed emotions. *Oh, God! Are You giving me a second chance?*

We worshipped and the presence of God flooded the place. One of our soloists sang passionately, a medley based around the life, death, and resurrection of Jesus. Her eyes closed as she belted out the words, "The blood will never lose its power ..."

I looked down at my notes, procrastinating. Of all Sundays. *There are a lot of new people here today. What am I going to do?*

As the lady sang, suddenly I heard a racket from the back

of the church. Laverne walked down the aisle toward me! She radiated joy as she flashed a bright smile around the place at the many people who knew her. I didn't do a thing! I walked toward her with a couple of the leaders, passing a church full of people worshipping God with all their hearts.

It was *all God.*

Like a Colorado forest fire, the news blazed through the community about Laverne and her miraculous healing.

Her immediate family had a lot of personal challenges and relationship issues. Next Sunday they came with Laverne to church. Eventually, all became believers in Jesus. The teens got involved in youth ministry, and her husband and the father helped out and supported us in the church. Their lives completely changed from the inside out.

I marveled at what God did, despite my lack of courage. I learned that when we don't know what to do, He will tell us. When He speaks, obey. And He gives second chances for His glory to perform. He loves people so

medication. Mom visited her after church.

When the doctors did rounds Monday, they had heard the rumors that something had happened to her over the weekend. On prior examinations they had pretty much written her off so if she said she was healed and could walk and wanted to go home they were not going to stop her. The doctors didn't believe her and watched her walk. She insisted on going home, but it took several hours to finalize paperwork.

Mom's best friend lived across from her family of seven (five kids). The healed lady and Mom became good friends and their family a part of our lives. They all came to church, even her husband who was an alcoholic, and I believe they all eventually gave their hearts to Jesus.

Paying it Forward in the Nations

Something very deep happened inside me that Easter Sunday. My faith expanded in my heart and I knew for certain that God could and would make miracles happen. I carried that with me through some very rough teenage years. And, overseas when I had opportunities to speak into people's lives prophetically and pray for healing.

On a mission trip with one of Pastor Russ's teams, Lana and I visited a woman in India who'd had a stroke and hadn't moved in four months. As I prayed for her, the Lord spoke to me and said, "Tell her to give you her hand." Without hesitation she picked up her hand and put it in mine.

Thinking that I was mistaken, I asked her to do it again and she did

continued...

then she cupped my hand and put it up to her face. Standing vigil at her beside, her family cried and praised the Lord—they'd not seen her move on her own in four months. We helped her sit on the edge of the bed and to stand, and we could see the muscles contracting in her thighs on their own. We put her back to bed unsure of how much she could endure because of fatigue and excitement and we left knowing the Holy Spirit had been fully present and that the Lord had healed her.

These healings are some of many times I've seen the Lord heal and completely change the course of peoples' lives. That seed of faith was planted when, as a small girl, I saw the lady on a bed in the back walk down the aisle of our church in her PJs.

much that He'll work even when we don't totally obey Him.

This was an incredible "faith boost" in the community and the church. When the news of the editor's healing began to circulate throughout the town, within a month we doubled in size. This miracle stirred up faith and new healings took place in the ministry. One miracle is worth more than much money spent on advertising—God will advertise His own workings and wonderful ways.

Through that newspaper editor's amazing healing and what I learned from my mistakes, I allowed the Lord to land more precious cargo in the form of spiritual insights and courage to take bold steps out of my comfort zone on the runways of my heart.

Flipped by the Spirit

As I became more knowledgeable of what the Scriptures teach, I led the congregation through a study in I Corinthians 12.

> There are diversities of gifts, but the same Spirit. There are differences of ministries, but the same Lord. And there are diversities of activities, but it is the same God who works all in all. But the manifestation of the Spirit is given to each one for the profit of all: for to one is given the *word of wisdom* through the Spirit, to another the *word of knowledge* through the same Spirit, to another *faith* by the same Spirit, to another the *gifts of healings* by the same Spirit, to another the *working of miracles,* to another *prophecy*, to another *discerning of spirits*, to another

different kinds of *tongues,* to another the *interpretation of tongues.* But one and the same Spirit works all these things, distributing to each one individually as He wills. (1 Corinthians 12:4–11, emphasis added)

I taught on the gifts of the Spirit in a class held prior to the Sunday morning service. I cited 1 Corinthians 14, Romans 8, Ephesians 5, and other passages during the Bible study those mornings.

We focused on *Jesus first* and *the gifts* second.

As only the Spirit can do, that particular gift or gifts I taught on manifested during the service that day—miracles, signs, and wonders like those by the hands of the apostles. People were coming into the flow of the Holy Spirit without even thinking about it.

One Sunday morning, we studied the gift of miracles.

"This is an intervention in the course of nature when the supernatural interrupts, suspends, halts, or ends the natural order of things." I surveyed the class and the people watching me with rapt attention. "Miracles are a release of power from the Holy Spirit to do something outside the range of human ability." *Yes! How exciting!* "They are *explosions* of the almightiness of an astonishing work of God that usually comes instantly." God uses miracles to get our attention and point to greater truths. He worked miracles by the hands of the apostles. Acts 5:12–16 says:

> And through the hands of the apostles many signs and wonders were done among the people. And they were all with one accord in Solomon's Porch. Yet none of the rest dared join them, but the people esteemed them highly. And believers were increasingly added to the Lord, multitudes of both men and women, so that they brought the sick out into the streets and laid them on beds and couches, that at least the shadow of Peter passing by might fall on some of them. Also a multitude gathered from the surrounding cities to Jerusalem, bringing sick people and those who were tormented by unclean spirits, and they were all healed.

Rita, one of our neighbors, walked into the church service that morning with her father—his first time ever—and they sat in the very front row. A hard and crusty man, Tom had been hurt by many preachers and was skeptical about God and church, so I was surprised to see him there. (The Holy Spirit draws people we'd never expect.)

"So when the power of God touches someone, sometimes unusual things happen, and each person responds differently," I said. "Some may fall. Some may fall to their knees. No human hands involved, the power of the Holy Spirit overcomes them. It is unexplainable, but it happens. Many things happen when people are out under the power of the Holy Spirit. Deliverance comes. Peace, joy, and happiness are released. Bondages are broken. Sometimes they have visions and dreams while lying on the floor as the Holy Spirit ministers to them. So much happens when you yield yourself to the workings of the Holy Spirit."

At the end of my message, Rita walked to the altar for prayer. Overcome by the Spirit before anybody could assist her, she gently fell to the floor, eyes closed.

Her father's mouth opened wide. He'd never seen anything like it before. "What's going on here?" he bellowed after the service.

"Tom, it's okay, it's okay." I assured him, looking at Rita peacefully lying there like she'd gone to another world. After a while, she opened her eyes and began to stretch and get up. A heavenly smile spread across her face.

The Lord imparted to that daughter of His a supernatural peace she'd never had before that operated in her life from that moment on.

"That Will Never Happen to Me!"

God definitely has a sense of humor.

Take my friend Jim, for instance. Jim and his wife were special people, and I'd married them. He was talented—both with handling horses and playing music. He had been a famous musician in Nashville, playing bass guitar with some of the great country western singers like Ricky Nelson. He was a proud man. And he'd adamantly scoff at the way people in our congregation sometimes shook uncontrollably and blubbered in an unknown tongue in the presence of the Holy Spirit.

Several times I watched as Jim slowly pulled a can of chewing tobacco out of the back pocket of his jeans, took a pinch and put it between his lips and gums. "That will *never* happen to me!"

I laughed at his comment. I'd heard this so many times, I wondered what the Lord might do to prove him wrong one day.

During a life group meeting in a trailer on a piece of land in the country one of our church members owned, I began to pray for people. Jim sauntered over to me for prayer. I reached out to lay my hand on his head. Just as I began to move my hand—I hadn't touched him—he fell suddenly to the floor! And his body wrapped around a chair. It was obvious this wasn't me or Jim doing this.

Remembering his vow he'd never let anything strange ever happen to *him*, several of the people in the trailer began to laugh as he lay on the floor, apparently knocked out.

"Look here at who got nailed!" One man slapped his knee and broke out in a fit of laughter.

"Ole Jim—said it would never happen to him!" another exclaimed between guffaws.

Jim later told me, "Brother Frase, I'll never forget how I said I'd never fall down! But before you even put your hand on me, I was gone on the floor and woke up under the chair." He paused. "Down there on the floor I felt the greatest peace I've ever had in my entire life."

A lot of people are afraid to enter into the Holy Spirit. But when the Holy Spirit works, God is always going to do something good. When we trust the Holy Spirit, He will keep things right. Not necessarily what you want it to be or plan it to be.

And Many Come

Baptists, Catholics, Methodists, Presbyterians, Lutherans, and people from other denominations pulled into our red dirt parking lot and walked through the doors onto the concrete of our humble building. Some were curious about what the Holy Spirit was doing in the lives of the people in our church. Some were hungry for more of the Lord. They'd go to their own churches on Sunday morning and come sit in our metal chairs in the evening and receive the baptism of the Holy Spirit. Many of them eventually understood the Holy Spirit better through the teaching and experiences in the services.

God performed many miracles and healings.

The word got out. Red dirt and all.

CHAPTER 14
Surprises in the Spirit

While we pastored New Life, Lana and I substitute taught high school in the Athens Independent School District for several years. We needed the money, but the Holy Spirit orchestrated this opportunity to also give us contacts with key educational figures and people throughout the city. We both taught elementary, sixth grade, and high school.

After we built our first sanctuary, seven public school teachers joined New Life Church. They begged me, "Please start a Christian school."

I did not feel the Holy Spirit leading in that direction. "No, this is not the time."

Four left the church, upset.

Soon we realized we had outgrown our first building—we needed a bigger "sheep shed."

After teaching a message on giving to jumpstart the project, a widow came to me after church.

"I've got a piece of land I am going to sell," she told me. "I feel the Lord wants me to give the money to the church."

Turns out, the land sold for $38,000. The seed for the new building.

At the same time, God was stirring my heart to start a kindergarten through 12th grade Christian school along with our building project. I had no idea where to begin—my 18-hour days left no room to start a school.

We fasted and prayed about the finances and timing for starting our new building. The numbers didn't add up—financially, it was totally impossible and crazy to build both.

Then Holy Spirit said, *Build them both now.*

We'd lost most of our teachers. And we didn't have enough money.

This doesn't make sense, Lord. A school, too?

Build both now, He repeated.

We had so many strikes against us. Besides not having teachers or money, we didn't have a vision for a school, and the deacons were against building both the new sanctuary and a school at the same time.

"That's too much," they told me.

"Well, I don't know what to say. The Lord spoke to me and told me we need to do it."

I felt a lot of external pressure from our members, but inwardly I felt a supernatural peace. Though circumstances told us this was the wrong thing at the wrong time, it was a supernatural gift of faith as recorded in 1 Corinthians 12:9: "To another [is given the gift of] faith by the same Spirit."

And then I called my friend at a nearby manufacturing company. He donated the rest of the money we needed to break ground.

That runway of my heart called "faith" turned out to be an unfinished gravel road. Not long after, still young in my walk with the Lord, I boldly stood before my congregation in a charismatic frenzy. "We are going to build this new building *debt free!*"

Almost everyone stood up as a roaring cheer reverberated around the sanctuary, putting electricity in the air. The financial fat was in the fire!

More funds poured in. The news on the streets: "The Baptist Pentecostals are building a new church debt-free!" But, before long, the funds dried up like Elijah's brook—with no ravens in sight. The steel was up, the roof on, window frames set.

And the wind blew through an empty building.

What began in faith became a fizzle—to some, "Frase's Folly."

We kept moving forward and paid off a 500-seat sanctuary—$250,000—in less than 3 years, establishing good credibility with our bank and vendors. I've learned in my five decades of ministry that sometimes we just do what we have to do and leave the rest with Him. Though we are not always faithful, God is.

Learning More about Trusting God for the Details

I'd asked the Lord, *If you will give me someone to run the school, I'll start one.*

George Williams, a retired engineer, surprised me one day as I was walking through the sanctuary. "If I can help you, Pastor, with the school, let me know."

"Yes, you can!"

My friend worked tirelessly and faithfully with me to complete the building project. He'd drive 40 miles to the church and home again late at night, fall out of the drivers' seat and crawl into his house, thoroughly exhausted.

He became a fast and dear friend, and I treasured the time we spent together.

Our teachers had moved to other places, so we needed new teachers. The Lord brought them to us—and we were ready with all but one, a fourth grade teacher.

A young mother showed up on the site and offered us iced tea in the hot summer sun. "What are you doing?"

We were digging a trench from the church to the water hookup on the street, covered with mud from head to toe. "Building a church and a Christian school." *And saving our church hundreds of dollars with this do-it-yourself project.*

"Really?" She looked at us quizzically. "Do you need teachers?"

I wiped some of the sweat and mud from my forehead and squinted up at her. "Yes."

"I teach fourth grade. Would you hire me?"

I looked at George who looked back at me, laughing. "Looks like God has given us our last teacher."

In a few months, along with the sanctuary, we built the school classrooms. We also assembled the school academically. We designed classes K–12, ordered the academic curriculums, created the application and registration process, hired the teachers, did all the promotion work of advertising in the community, conducted an orientation, prepared the classrooms for the new teachers, built a playground. *And* communicated the process to the church for a good buy-in.

There were a number of disgruntled ones who thought we shouldn't turn over our new facilities to a bunch of destructive kids. But we pushed forward and sometime around 1978, we opened the school.

As I stood before the congregation the last Wednesday evening before we moved into our new sanctuary with the new school, I sensed the Holy

Spirit wanted to move in a special way. Accustomed to His changing winds, I sensed Him wooing many to come to Christ.

One person walked toward me at the altar. Then another. Then another. Thirteen people gave their hearts and lives to Jesus in a service I'll never forget.

It was a monumental sign for the congregation: a harbinger of what would come the days ahead in our new building. In the next 10 years, we baptized more than 1,000 converts.

It pays to allow the Holy Spirit do His work.

A School of Excellence

Our school became well-known in the community for its spirit of excellence in education. Because of word-of-mouth testimonies, public school representatives showed up in our classrooms to find out what we were doing.

Also, many of the students from the community accepted Jesus into their lives and started coming to New Life Church with their parents, who also got saved.

One year, the last day of school before a Thanksgiving break, we showed the film *Pilgrim's Progress*. When it ended, 24 of the children came to the front of the room, and I led them in a saving knowledge of Jesus Christ. The vision of those eager young eyes fixed on me, and the sense of those tiny beating hearts ready for their new life in Christ has remained with me clearly to this day. That's how the Holy Spirit is. He gives us things we'll always remember.

> One of the easiest ways to know if the Holy Spirit is moving in your congregation is when your heart starts to expand beyond your borders by loving and praying for those you don't know (1 John 2:6–9).

Building the new sanctuary and school ushered in a new season of ministry for us that lasted a decade. Besides water baptizing many people, we helped those from many different denominations experience the baptism of the Holy Spirit and a greater understanding of the gifts the Lord landed on the runways of eager, open hearts.

Parking Lot Prayers for
Other Churches and Our Own Revival

One of my dear church members gave our family a red Volkswagen. For several years every Sunday morning before the service, I climbed into that Volkswagen at 6:00 a.m. and drove to the parking lots of many churches and prayed for the pastor of that church. Episcopalian. Presbyterian. Methodist. Catholic. These pastors and priests were all men I had come to know and care about through the ministerial alliance in town.

It took me an hour or two before I headed for my own church. By the time I arrived at New Life, I carried with me a spirit of revival! The Lord dropped sometimes as many as 10 words of knowledge into my heart for our people.

When we started worshipping, I released those words into the congregation.

"Someone needs healing in their shoulder."

"Someone here has been discouraged and is looking for direction in your life. The Lord would like you to know that thing in your heart is from Him. Act on it!"

"Someone here has just been diagnosed with cancer."

"Come to the altar if you feel these words are for you, and we'll pray for you."

They came and we were in a great spiritual flow even before the service began.

One Sunday, the Holy Spirit spoke strongly to me about spirits of suicide.

"There are those here who have been contemplating suicide. The Lord wants you to know that He loves you very much. And He is going to turn around the situations that are giving you deep anxiety right now. He wants to deliver others from depression that is oppressing you so much you want to take your own life. Come to the altar and be delivered!"

Several streamed to the front and received prayer and deliverance from their torment.

"Look at this report!" a church member waved papers in front of me. A cancer diagnosis and clean bill of health. The cancer had vanished, to the surprise of the medical staff.

Praying Catholic Ladies and Their Priest

Precious Catholic ladies came Sunday nights. Some of them were filled with the *more* of the Holy Spirit. One Sunday night, they came running up the aisle to me. "Father Frase! Father Frase! Did you hear about Father Tucek?"

"Oh, yeah. He got baptized with the Holy Spirit with evidence of speaking in tongues."

"How did you know?"

This news didn't surprise me. "I've been praying for him for a year for that very thing."

This occurred simultaneously with the outpouring of the charismatic renewal of the 70s that swept through the Catholic Church. There is no end to what the Holy Spirit can accomplish through prayer when people join together as a mighty force on earth, yielding to God and His work.

The Holy Spirit taught us more about Himself daily as we sought Him. He established the people of New Life and in the community in the gifts of the Spirit, growing us in a fresh understanding of how He can do anything through each of us.

Skeptic Sprinklers

A dear Methodist family began to visit our services.

"We've already been baptized," one said, planting his feet firmly in front of me.

I tried to let out some of the tension. "What was it like?"

"We were sprinkled with water when we were babies."

"Okay, if you feel that was a good thing, that's fine," I affirmed. I shared what we believed—that baptism under water is a symbol of letting go of the old life and coming out of the water is rising to new life in Christ.

They kept coming back to church and probably saw some of our baptisms. One day they approached me and said, "We'd like to be water baptized—*under* the water! We see that it is biblical."

One by one, I dunked these "sprinkled Methodists" under the water. They popped up with water splashing all around and big grins on their faces.

We saw so many people whose lives were changed by biblical truths.

The Cowboy Dunk

One Sunday night at New Life, we planned to baptize 42 people—which was quite a few people for our little town. We crowded into the new building that seated 500. People stood along the walls. Even though rumors circulated around town that "there are snakes under Pastor Frase's pulpit!" that's actually where the baptistery was.

As we baptized new believers, the spiritual intensity built as dozens of people stepped into the water and came out dripping and smiling. At the end, I asked, "Is there anyone else out there who would like to follow Jesus in baptism?"

We'd been praying for a tall, redheaded cowboy for months. His wife came to church at New Life, and I'd baptized his children that night.

I heard a loud rustle in the congregation, then the cowboy jumped up and pulled his boots off and tossed them aside. With his watch on his wrist and his wallet in his pocket, he jumped right into the water right beside me.

After my shock wore off, I dunked him under the water and brought him up again, spraying us both with the public symbol of his new life in Christ.

Full Gospel Men and Women's Aglow

In the thick of things, we were a driving force for the Charismatic movement in our community, including the surrounding towns. Reaching out to draw ordinary businessmen together to share their testimonies of faith in their work with a belief in the full range of gifts of the Spirit, we started a local chapter of the Full Gospel Businessmen. We also reached out to women in the community by starting a Women's Aglow chapter in Athens. Now known as simply Aglow and embracing men as well, according to its website, it "is an apostolic voice bringing a biblical perspective to the governmental, economic, and social issues of our time."

It really pumped me to initiate cooperation among people in the community from various denominations and encourage them to become involved and grow spiritually.

My Sermon Cast Aside for The Holy Spirit's 12 Prophecies

One Wednesday evening service I learned a great lesson on listening to and obeying the Holy Spirit. I walked to the pulpit with a prepared message—I always prepared well. As I stepped up, I sensed a prophetic word coming from the Holy Spirit. I closed my notebook and delivered the word.

When I finished, I felt the wind of the Spirit move upon me again and here came another prophetic word, which I spoke out. My congregation watched with surprise and rapt attention. I took a deep breath, reached for my notes, but there came another prophecy.

The tangible presence of the Lord filled the air, like a growing breeze filling the sails of a small boat on a vast blue lake.

I waited.

Another word came, and it was obvious to the people and me that we were under a divine visitation.

Then the Holy Spirit descended upon me, and His presence grew and grew in and around all of us. It felt like the wind whipping up whitecaps all around as the sun streamed through the clouds and the boat picked up speed, splashing through the breaking swells. The people lifted their eyes and arms upward and worshipped in the midst of that swirling Holy Spirit wind, and we melted into its power as it surrounded us.

Twelve words came through me, each more glorious than the one before. I realized that there'd be no message from Pastor Russ that evening. It was all Him and His glory, not sought or drummed up by my spirit.

These prophetic words were given specifically for our congregation.

That ministry moment lives on in my heart. More and more I realize how the Holy Spirit has an agenda that trumps our own. We have to learn to listen and obey.

A fresh word or words from God at an important time encourages our souls and can set the course for new direction.

The Biker Couple Reappears

Around 1980, we began a third building project: our Family Life Center and gymnasium. During that time, a young man I'd mentored in our church asked me to preach at a revival in his church in Palestine, Texas. He'd attended Bible school in San Antonio and served on the mission field for a while.

I preached several nights to a crowd of 150 in their rented building, packed and overflowing with the glory of God and His heavy presence. While worshipping on the stage one night, I glanced at the crowd and who should I see but Beverly and Chase, the bikers! I hadn't seen them in years. After Beverly was healed of the sleeping disease and tattooed mean-dude Chase was saved in his home, they attended New Life church a while with their two children. Then they abruptly left town.

The couple slipped into the aisle and moved near the stage to reunite with me. In the midst of the crowd worshipping, we embraced one another with hugs and joyful tears. It was a happy reunion!

> **The word of knowledge unlocks a pain in a person's life**. So often this gift is used poorly for the benefit of the speaker, or some people make up the words to impress the crowds. When it comes from the Father through the Holy Spirit it's intention is to heal and restore.

Supernatural Word of Knowledge for a Teen Girl

Children came forward and sat on the stage. Seven or eight kids sat on both sides of the stage, watching and listening.

I noticed a thin black girl with the youth—a teenager about 14 with curly, short hair. She walked up to me in the thick of the moving of the Spirit. As I looked at her, in my mind I saw a disturbing vision of her as a little girl.

"You are walking behind a bicycle … with a rope tied around your neck."

Her head went down and she began sobbing.

"And there is a big person riding the bicycle, pulling you along."

"Th–that's my daddy!" she said in shame. "When I did something wrong, he would tie a rope around my neck and pull me down the street."

White hankies dotted the crowd as people pulled them out, sniffling in the midst of a heavy presence of God's love.

"Well, God wants you to know that He is your heavenly Father, and unlike your earthly father, He doesn't want to shame or punish you." I touched her shiny black curls as the tears rolled down her cheeks.

"He loves you deeply and is so grieved by what your father did to you. Your heavenly Father is pleased with you. He delights in you!"

Her shoulders shook as she sobbed.

Many knew this girl, knew what I did not know about her before God's supernatural wisdom flowed through me. It seems like they'd not heard such a specific word of knowledge like this before, and everything broke loose. I heard loud crying and saw tears streaming down faces all around me. Hands raised as freedom broke out in the service. Words of knowledge flowed forth, and the Lord ministered to many, giving them prophetic words of encouragement for their lives.

Several moved to the stage and gave their hearts to Christ.

It was one of those nights you never forget. The service went on and on.

Afterward, I looked for Chase and Beverly, but they'd disappeared— again. I never saw them or heard from them after that.

CHAPTER 15

Living Where God Chooses

"I'm flying you in to attend Israel Awareness Day—a big deal—at our church!" Burl Outlaw's voice boomed over the phone one sunny day in 1982. I'd led Burl to the Lord in Athens, and he'd moved to Denver, Colorado, a year or two earlier. He'd become successful in the oil and gas business.

"Okay …" I soon discovered this was a huge annual event at Faith Bible Chapel (FBC) in Arvada, Colorado. Jewish folks are invited to honor Israel with Christians who love and stand with Israel.

We stayed for four to five days. Bob Hooley was the senior pastor. George Morrison and I greeted one another in the hallway briefly. George, an associate pastor at the time, told me later that when we shook hands, the Holy Spirit whispered to him, *Someday you two will be working together.*

My family liked Colorado, and we planned a family vacation to visit again the next year. In the summer of 1983 Lana, Paula (12), Rusty (8), and I drove to Colorado near Denver. I drank in the cool air spraying off the mountain streams while the kids joyfully skipped rocks and shouted when they saw trout resting in the side pools. And Lana kept her eye on us as she stirred the fire for hot dogs.

In 1984, Burl flew us to Israel—a place I'd always wanted to visit—on a trip with FBC. We joined Burl, Carol Hooley, and Cheryl Morrison (who directed Israel and Women's Ministries at the church). She and Pastor George traveled to Israel, usually leading teams and a group of mostly teens—the International Singers and Dancers—who performed for the Israeli military every year. They visited Israel more than 50 times before they retired from pastoring the church in January 2017.

Truthfully, Lana had never desired to visit Israel. She tired of sitting in a dark room viewing "Holy Land slides." A Southern lady of diverse tastes, she preferred traveling to exotic places: standing beneath the engineered magnificence of the tallest free-standing tower in the world, Paris's Eiffel Tower; or floating in a gondola down one of Venice's canals meandering around its vast collection of islands and bridges and romantic ancient-walled buildings.

Cheryl and Carol's connections led us to make friends with our Israeli guides and spend time mingling with some of the hospitable Jewish folks of the land of Israel, with their rich religious traditions, kosher foods, and warm hearts. Lana fell in love with the people and that holy place. In fact, one night after we returned, I glanced over my menu in a restaurant to see her eyes filling with tears.

"What's the matter?" I asked.

"I miss Israel!" she said.

I glanced around at the people eating at tables around us with mock impatience. "Stop crying! People will think we are fighting!"

But I understood exactly how she felt.

Pastor George Morrison's Invitation

In 1985, Pastor Hooley resigned and Pastor George became senior pastor for Faith Bible Chapel. Pastor George asked us if we would consider moving to Denver to plant a new church: Faith Bible Chapel Southwest in Littleton. It never occurred to me that we'd leave New Life. For 10 years we'd lived adventurously in the book of Acts with great spiritual success and activity, adding on to our original building with a Family Life Center and gym, building a new sanctuary and K-12 classrooms—and we were completely out of debt. Anyone would be crazy to leave that.

Pastor George flew to Dallas to talk with me more about it. I can only imagine what he thought when I picked him up in a black Lincoln Continental as long as a city block! A widow had sold us that car out of her barn. Pastor George later told me he thought as he stepped into the Lincoln, *Russ is rich! He'll never leave Texas and come to Denver.*

But we spent several days talking about the possibility of Lana and me planting a new church. It was the most difficult decision we had ever faced.

With our lives and hearts embedded in a community of friends, we couldn't leave without knowing it was God's plan. We'd be leaving behind a lot of broken hearts. The people had invested their lives and pocketbooks and poured their money into expanding our campus several times. But I also had a nagging, unsettling feeling that many did not want to mature in ways the Lord wanted to take them and the church.

The seeds you sow on Sunday are being pulled up on Monday, the Holy Spirit whispered to me one day. *They won't let you take them any further.*

At a prophetic gathering in the country in a friend's barn, the late prophet John Paul Jackson, who knew nothing about our situation, called out Lana and me from the crowd. "You are in a hot air balloon," he said to us, "and there are people holding the ropes, holding you back from God's divine purpose." (Through decades of ministry his prophetic words were incredibly accurate for people.)

A few weeks later, while sitting on the stage at our church, Lana saw in a vision an overgrown potted plant, and that the plant needed to be replanted into a bigger pot.

I earnestly sought the Lord. *Have we gone as far as we can go with our New Life family? Is this the necessary ending for a new beginning?* I pondered these things in my heart, like Mary, mother of Jesus, when the angel visited her and told her she would birth Jesus, the Son of God.

As beautiful and wonderful as people are, sometimes there comes a time in a ministry when those you lead quit listening to you and following you. At the same time, I also realized that I didn't have the leadership maturity to take these precious children of God to higher levels of maturity where they needed to go. I didn't have mentors surrounding me to show me that I was *doing, doing, doing* for the people 18 hours a day rather than teaching others what they could do and delegating to them. I didn't have mentors to ask me the tough questions, like, was I spending enough time with my wife? Or taking care of my family first?

God knew that much of what I needed in order to grow awaited me in Denver with the staff at Faith Bible Chapel and the connection with other pastors in Colorado. The Lord wanted to lead this fish to a larger pond, surrounded by more mature fish who could teach me how to develop a ministry team, influence them, and delegate—rather than trying to do so much myself.

After several months of agonizing over the decision of whether to move to Denver or not, in November 1985, we sensed God's plan in it. We packed up our family and belongings and headed for new adventures that awaited us in Arvada.

Rather than sticking with the few runways I was previously operating on—and content with—I surrendered and trusted the Lord as He increased the number of runways in my heart. And in taking the risk, discovered more precious cargo the Holy Spirit wanted to land on them as we said "Yes!" to moving north.

We did not know the future, but I knew that our Air Traffic Controller could see everything and would guide us through the shifting wind currents, give us new insights and show us higher vistas. I kept my eyes glued on the radar and my ears attuned to His changing frequency on my internal radio as I "piloted our plane" from Texas to Colorado.

CHAPTER 16

Expanding Runways: On Staff in Colorado

Pastor George shared the plan: I'd join Faith Bible Chapel in Arvada in 1985 as an associate pastor, become part of the team there, catch their vision, and then plant Faith Bible Chapel Southwest (FBCSW) in Littleton, Colorado, in a couple of years.

With this move came a new level of opportunity for my own spiritual maturity. In Texas, serving relentlessly as an 18-hour-a-day pastor, I'd taken good care of people, but did not serve them well by not delegating or helping them move into areas of ministry where they could grow, enabling me to spend more time in the areas God had gifted me. But now, in Colorado, I became part of a staff and opportunities opened for me to receive mentoring. I learned more about leadership, and delegation deepened my understanding of how to allow what I received from the Lord on the runways of my heart to spill over onto others in a healthy and natural way.

A few months after my family arrived and settled in Arvada, the people living in southwest Denver told Pastor George, "If you brought Pastor Russ here to start a church, why wait for two years? We want one now!"

So, three months after we arrived, we held home meetings in Phil and Marge Kaspar's basement. With the support of Faith Bible Chapel, other pastors, and a teamwork mentality, our church rapidly outgrew the basement and moved to a facility at Coalmine and Wadsworth, officially launching FBC Southwest in 1986. No longer shouldering the responsibilities of a church by myself, I reveled in the growth of a new and exciting congregation. I became surer of the giftings God had given me, and we grew in the Spirit-led and Spirit-filled life.

We met for daily prayer at 6:00 a.m., a discipline I'd done for years at New Life. I laid this prayer foundation in our church after reading Dr. Larry Lea's pivotal book, *Could You Not Tarry One Hour? Learning the Joy of Prayer*. It centered on praying the Lord's Prayer ("Our Father, who art in Heaven …").

At the time, we lived in Arvada while pastoring FBCSW in Littleton, so I had to leave early every morning and drive 30 minutes to join the others.

One morning, running late (which I hate), a policeman caught me speeding before I turned into the church's parking lot. Wouldn't you know, with his red-and-blue lights flashing, he followed me right up to the curb and jumped out of his squad car. He stopped me in front of the glassed-in room where the members prayed!

"I got ya!" he said. "What's your hurry?"

"See that group of people in there?" I pointed to the window where several faces watched us, smirking. "They are praying, and I'm late."

"Okay. I'm giving you just a warning this time …" He backed off, trying to hide a smile on his face.

As I entered the room, the people waiting roared.

The Gift of Discernment

First Corinthians 12:10 states, "To another [member of the church is given] discerning of spirits." This discernment is critical in this day and time. It is insight from God to see into the unseen realm of the spirit world to know what is going on spiritually beneath the surface of a matter. It is the spiritual impartation to discern or distinguish between the spirit of Satan and that of the Holy Spirit, between demonic spirits and the human spirit. It gives us the ability to know the difference between the counterfeit and the truth.

The Apostle Paul dealt with this. An example in the Scripture is in Acts 16:16–18. Paul and his fellow workers were preaching in the streets and a lady—a fortune teller possessed by a demonic spirit, a spirit of divination— who made much money for her masters with this spirit, followed them down the street, mocking them day after day. "These men are servants of the Most High God …"

Paul, greatly annoyed, discerned this unholy spirit and said to it, "I command you in the name of Jesus to come out of her." The spirit left at that very hour, and she could no longer do what she'd been doing. Her masters, of course, were very angry. Their hope of profit left with the spirit.

We need the discerning of spirits in our lives to know what is of God and what is of the devil.

Confusion in a Service and the Gift of Discernment

Something very odd occurred in our service one Sunday morning. Faith Bible Chapel Southwest, now numbering about 100 to 150 people, met in a high school auditorium. We were still new and I was learning who people were. One Sunday morning, as the service started, everything was out of sync—the piano player, the musicians, and the order of service. My cup of water on the stand I used for my Bible turned over in my lap and soaked me.

As we sang, I heard a voice inside me like a wind say, *Get all of the people out of the church. The roof is going to fall in. Here you are a young new pastor, and if you don't get them out, they'll die.*

The voice mixed with the confusion that surrounded us. I'd learned that where there's confusion, there's demonic activity or witchcraft.

I called all the people down to the altar and said, "Hey, folks! We've got confusion here in the spirit realm and witchcraft activity. I'm not sure where it's coming from, but we need to pray."

Heaven came down and filled us with a spirit of peace as everyone gathered at the altar worshipping and praying. As we prayed and worshipped, the confusion broke and people got saved. We later learned that at the very moment of breakthrough, a member of our church—who suffered in the hospital—also received a breakthrough. We found out this lady ate her first solid meal in 10 years!

After the service, I learned what had happened. Ushers didn't tell me at the time because they didn't understand what was going on. Later, they explained that two women we didn't know came in and sat in the back, making signs with their hands and saying strange things. We believe they were witches incanting spells on the service. When I called people to the front to pray, they ran out of the service.

The Lord had given me discernment not to listen to the voice that told me to send people out of the auditorium, but to call upon the Lord to dispel the confusion. We ended up having a great service with mighty works of God manifested.

Waiting on the Lord to Minister as a Body

On Wednesday nights, I encouraged everyone to come to the altar. We'd worship and prophesy, get words of knowledge, and minister to one another.

Dave Wurtsbaugh, a dear friend and elder, worked construction, lifting bricks and concrete. His back constantly went out on him. I didn't realize at the time, but he hurt so much, he lay on the floor at home, crying.

One night when he worshipped with us, I sensed the Lord wanted to heal someone with a bad back. "Something is wrong with your vertebras," I called out for someone in the congregation.

Dave raised his hand. He moved closer and I prayed for him. I didn't know until two or three years later that his spine corrected and his pain disappeared.

"Remember that time you prayed for me?" he mentioned one time when we were together.

"Yeah! Yeah!"

"I got healed that night!"

Prophetic Word that Moved a Teenager into His Destiny

One Sunday, the Holy Spirit spoke to me to prophesy over all the teenagers. One of the teens, Matt Haley, recorded the word, typed it, and framed this directive. I read it later at his Eagle Scout installation. He hung it on his dorm wall in college and now it hangs on his law office wall, a testimony to God's spoken plan for him that directed him through those years.

Another Sunday, I heard the Holy Spirit's whisper: *Prophesy over every church member.*

Every church member, Lord? That will take forever! And will I have a word from You for every single one?

I encouraged people to line up and began to go down the line. As soon as I stood in front of a person, something would come to mind, and I spoke it out. When I finally got to the last lady, nothing came to me. So I didn't say anything.

Later, in the car, Lana teased, "That was one of my favorite ladies! Of all the people you didn't have a prophecy for!"

I've learned that if the Holy Spirit is not giving me anything, better to be silent than make something up.

Entering a New Season

FBCSW moved several times as we grew into a young, vibrant "Word and Spirit" congregation of 300. We established the FBC School of the Bible and reached into our community. Many were born again and the gifts of the Spirit were released by the people.

On New Year's Day in 1989, I sensed a rumbling in my spirit. *A big change is coming. So much* more *is coming …*

CHAPTER 17

Rocky Mountain Bible Institute

Faith Bible Chapel Southwest was flourishing, and Pastor George and the elders were very pleased with the progress. Around 1987, at a staff meeting, Pastor George said to me, "I really feel like we need to start an accredited Bible school."

I nodded. "I'll help you find the right people."

A few months later, we passed each other in the hall of the administrative offices one day. "I really want to start a Bible school that will prepare young men and women for the ministry," he said, half to himself, but glancing at me.

"I know some educators who could do such a thing," I offered. He didn't follow up and ask for references from me.

I'd laid out a ten-year plan for growth for our church in the SW Metro Denver area. As I prayed on January 1, 1990, the Holy Spirit whispered to me, *Put the plan away as this will be a year of change.* I did not tell Pastor George about that.

Another Runway of Opportunity Opens

Some time later, Pastor George and I headed for lunch with six of our pastors. As the two of us walked together toward the restaurant, he told me resolutely, "I'm ready to start a Bible college. And I want *you* to do it! You will have to leave your church to do this. It will take you full time."

The Holy Spirit had prepared me for this moment, and though I'd been looking forward to building FBCSW, my heart flooded with fresh expectation. I knew it was the right time to move in a new direction.

A desire returned that I'd had back in Athens and had forgotten. We'd bought land near the church to build a Bible school campus not long before God called our family to Denver. That desire to start a Bible school had been simmering deep inside for a long time. But the Frase family moved before we could follow through. Now, the Lord planned to make good on that desire. Pastor George had sensed God's timing to start a Bible school connected with Faith Bible Chapel, and that I should be one to pilot the program.

One of the vital lessons I have learned through these 50 years: the Holy Spirit is always right on time—and it is up to me to listen and obey when the new runway in my heart is challenged to open. The Holy Spirit knows what we don't and, if we walk in step with the Spirit, He will position our plane on the right runway ready to take off!

After we talked about the Bible college, Pastor George and I walked into the restaurant that day for lunch with the pastors, filled to the brim with great expectations as we shared the vision of Faith Bible Chapel opening an accredited Bible college. I'd pastored the church in southwest Denver for six years, but that season would soon end.

I'd met Dr. Dannie Fisher at Southwestern Baptist Seminary in Fort Worth. His young family and mine got together quite a few times. When FBC needed another pastor, I had connected him with Pastor George, and the Fishers moved to Colorado. He was now one of the pastors at the lunch, and he graciously agreed to pastor Faith Bible Chapel Southwest, releasing me to the new path. Though it happened quickly, Pastor George had been praying and thinking about it for quite a while.

Not only was the Lord opening a runway of *more* in my life but the opportunity to impact others who desired deeper training and equipping for missions expanded as well.

"Okay, go do it!" is pretty much what Pastor George and the elders said. As the reality of a new role as educator sank in, I shook in my boots. *I'm not trained to educate, but to preach, pastor, and make disciples of Jesus.* I felt like Mary, mother of Jesus, when the angel gave her the assignment of birthing God Almighty in the flesh. Pretty heady stuff. Then the angel left her to birth the baby.

FBC leadership entrusted me with Rocky Mountain Bible Institute, and I didn't have a clue what to do.

Learning the Accreditation Process for RMBI

I resigned from Faith Bible Chapel Southwest Church in June 1991, remaining on staff with FBC. The next 15 months, Lana and I crisscrossed the country, visiting as many schools as we could, gathering necessary information and completing the paperwork we needed to launch RMBI in the fall of 1992.

During that time, I heard that Oral Roberts University in Tulsa, Oklahoma, was hosting a conference on how to receive accreditation for schools. We realized it would posture the school we wanted to create with a greater advantage if our students could transfer credits into higher institutes of learning.

Go to this event, I heard the Holy Spirit whisper.

A gnawing sense of inadequacy crept in as I looked around the crowd of 50 leaders in a glassed-in room of the Oral Roberts Prayer Tower. I thought, *What a highly educated bunch of folks!*

"The goal of accreditation is to ensure that institutions of higher education meet acceptable levels of quality," the speaker began. "Accreditation in the United States involves nongovernmental entities as well as federal and state government agencies. Since those of you attending this conference have been in operation for at least two years, we will first address ..."

I looked up and down my row at the men and women as they watched this speaker with rapt attention. *We haven't even had our first class ... I'm in the right place, but at the wrong time.*

At break time, I introduced myself to the convener, Dr. Petry, and told him our situation.

"Oh, Brother Frase, that's just fine! Stay with us through the conference, and it will be advantageous for you in the process."

Relieved, I took the accreditation notebook he handed me. Flipping through it, I realized it laid out the whole process—perfect!

Besides meeting new peers, I knew we needed to do this.

The information from this conference propelled us forward quickly into the accreditation process. The Holy Spirit will always prepare us for future advancement as we occupy ourselves in what He is currently doing in our well-chosen courses. I'll always value the support of Pastor George, the FBC elders, and a team of great players behind me all the way, especially in the accreditation process. RMBI was accredited in two years—unheard of.

Shortly thereafter, I was invited to serve as a national accrediting chairman for Oral Roberts University's International Christian Accrediting Association and traveled to help other schools become accredited.

This process prepared me well for the next season of my life, as God dug out new runways for us and others He called.

First Semester at RMBI

With great anticipation, on that first day of classes in Fall 1992, I opened the door to one of our classrooms long before the students would arrive. The early dawn sunlight sent beams through the slotted blinds. Soon 30 students would walk through the doorway into a new realm of learning and opportunity. I laid hands on each seat, praying earnestly.

Lord, teach these students what You want them to know. Call them forth to a place of ministry. And this slipped from my mouth. *Or to the nations!*

With fear and trembling, as I cried out to God, I wondered what kind of venture this would be. *Will we be able to do this? Will it fail or will it succeed?*

My knees buckled at one of the desks. I looked at the doorway. *Is it too late to run out?* I looked around at the little classroom picturing those 30 students all looking up at me, pens in hand, tapping them on their desks. Expecting from me. Enrolling because they would learn here.

Hadn't I seen God's hand in every step leading up to this place? Weeks ago, I was so sure that we were doing the right thing and confident that the school would successfully train these students for great things. But now …

I'm not equipped for this …

I stood up, took a deep breath, and adjusted my collar. I looked out the slotted blinds where the sunbeams lightened and strengthened in their shining path into the room.

I am obeying the Lord. He is behind this. He will see us through. This will be an exciting journey—for all of us!

The students began to trickle into the room, some laughing and talking, some quiet and thoughtful. An assortment of people from several churches.

"Hello!" My son, Rusty, waved at me. I'd talked it over with him and impressed upon him that he didn't have to enroll for my sake. I wanted him to make his own well-thought-out decision. And, there he was. I anticipated his participation each day that first semester with great joy.

Okay … here we go!

Students from the First Class Teach *Me*

Two days later, a kid from Thailand came up to me after class to talk. He'd been struggling with his classwork.

"Dean Frase …" Aje's eyes darted to the side, and he took a deep breath. "Dean Frase, I am having a hard time," he said in broken English. "When you talk, I have to take your English and translate it into my language—the Akha language—and then translate it into English. All very quickly, before you say your next sentence." He looked away again. "Could you … could you please speak a bit more slowly?"

A few weeks later, several of the students wanted to meet with me. They marched into my office and stood in front of my desk. I wasn't sure what they had on their minds.

The bravest, tallest one spoke. "Dean Frase, if you are going to reach our generation, you are going to have to learn how to teach."

Gulp.

The runway of humility opened wide in front of me, inviting me to taxi onto it. I'd worked 15 to 18 hours a day developing this school, traveling all over America to observe and investigate many schools. I was even simultaneously earning my doctor of ministry online from Luther Rice University in Atlanta, Georgia, and writing my dissertation topic on the "Creation and Implementation of a Theological Institute for a Local New Testament Church." Very intellectual.

And yet, in one nanosecond, my students dismantled my ability, courage, and confidence in the classroom!

For days I agonized over that meeting. Tears streamed down my face, and depression crowded out my excitement and hope. *I'm a failure. What am I trying to do at RMBI?*

One day, as I agonized about my shortcomings, the Holy Spirit said, *I didn't call you to teach. I called you to impart to these students. Model Jesus. Pour out of you and into the students all that you've learned from Me through the years to empower them to get where I want them to go.*

Impartation is the spiritual transference of the Holy Spirit, the release from one person to another. Like Moses, who laid hands on 70 leaders. And Elijah's mantle that fell onto Elisha, imparting to him a double measure of the Spirit to Elisha.

Impart! Help them move forward. Yes! That seemed easier than teaching for me. *I can do that, for sure!*

I got smart and hired good teachers. For the next 14 years, I gave my spirit, body, and soul to the task of raising up men and women for ministry and the Great Commission, stirring up passion in students for walking in the gifts and serving the Lord, semester after semester. And graduating them—many flew to places around the world as missionaries, church planters, apostles, prophets, evangelists, and pastor-teachers.

I learned so much and matured in those years at RMBI. I enjoyed working with those eager to learn God's Word and His ways. And, as a bonus, I learned a few things about teaching along the way.

Everyone needs a runway lined with other saints whose experience can light the way, mature them, and move them into yet greater levels of influence and effectiveness. I received that and passed it on to the RMBI students also by inviting missionary mentors to speak and giving them materials to read.

Two years after starting RMBI, in 1994, I earned my doctorate from Luther Rice.

God knew He was laying the groundwork for something more far-reaching than one Bible college in Colorado. Something I would not realize until years later.

Highlights of My Years of RMBI

It's impossible to express all that happened during those years I served as dean of Rocky Mountain Bible Institute. Probably the greatest thing is how it educated me and matured me into a better leader. Running the school blessed me with many wonderful students who are now world changers, quite a few of whom I minister with today. Often I hear from former students who went on to secular pursuits, "RMBI was the best two years of my life!"

It also prepared me for the greatest time of fruitfulness of my life after RMBI.

Before the semester started, teachers and students gathered in Estes Park, Colorado, for a special time to get to know one another, to

See in
PART TWO: More Stories
"Runways of the
RMBI Graduates to the Nations"
for the impact those students are
making around the world.

pray together, fellowship, and for me to prophesy over the students. These awesome retreats of refreshing and flow of the Spirit established the school year in spiritual concrete. God significantly marked the lives of many for future ministry during these retreats.

We graduated about 500 RMBI students from 1992 to 2005. The Holy Spirit moved and ministered in ways beyond what I could have thought of or imagined.

A few of the memorable stories include:

1. **The scientist with a PhD who couldn't read.**

   "Dean Frase, I can't do this!" he told me one early morning in my office.
   "You have a PhD—what do you mean?"
   "I did all that without reading a book," he said, with genuine tears.
   "You can *do* it!" I told him.
   He did excellent work and joyfully graduated.

2. **The businessman who sold his business to attend RMBI, but with a problem.**

   He'd come to RMBI to receive training to enter the mission field. I looked up as he walked into my office with a sober look on his face. "I can't do this. I haven't written a paper since high school. I can't take a test."
   "Yes, you can. Soon you'll be doing 'A' work," I told him confidently.
   He rose to the task and aced the course.

3. **The girl whose life took a dramatic turn.**

A student brought a guest to chapel one day. At the end before we dismissed, this guest let out a blood-curdling scream and was thrown to the floor by a demon spirit. Everybody in the room froze. Nervously, I knelt over her and cast out the demon, setting her free. She not only gave her life to Jesus, but she also became an RMBI student and graduated to go on and help others.

4. **The successful attorney who "lost it."**

A distinguished man of great means, he wore a suit and bow tie to class. Older than our 19-year-old students, his congenial and gracious spirit won my heart.

"Everything we read about in Leviticus," I told the class, "the animal and grain sacrifices and offerings the Jewish people made, Jesus accomplished on the cross at Calvary. It is now 'finished.' All we need to do is accept that finished work."

I noticed the attorney's face was bright red as tears flowed down his cheeks.

Oh, my! I thought. *This is a God moment!*

He raised his hand, and sobbing, he said, "You mean Jesus did all that on the cross so we wouldn't have to?"

"Yes."

That "well put-together" lawyer cried his way into the saving grace of God.

5. **The student from a difficult family with nothing to his name.**

He worked hard to graduate and came to me after graduation with his plan.

"Dean Frase, I am going to the Philippines to be a missionary."

Though a great guy with strong determination, his challenges were big.

"How will you get there?" I asked.

"I have money for half my ticket cost," he told me.

I looked into his resolute face, sensed his heart, and took out my checkbook. I wrote a check for the rest. "I believe in you."

The RMBI graduate lived as a successful missionary in the Davao and Cebu regions in the Philippines for 20 years. I ministered with him and the YWAM students at the base there on occasion.

After he had established the ministry and returned to the States on furlough, I invited him to teach and prophesy in the chapel. "When Dean Frase said, 'I believe in you,' those words encouraged me," he told the current students. "Those prophetic words moved me into my gifting as a missionary and launched me into my calling."

My former student then prophesied over all the students and encouraged them in their callings, and he was incredibly accurate. The Lord planned an amazing destiny for this young man while attending RMBI, and the Holy Spirit brought it to fruition.

Students to the Nations

RMBI served as a sending entity for Faith Bible Chapel, and students enrolled from nations overseas. Some went on to graduate from other institutes with bachelor's and master's degrees, and even PhDs. So many of the students were launched into ministry in the US and throughout the world after they received training at RMBI.

And, little did I realize God would bring many of them back to me for an even greater, more fruitful work He had in mind in the nations.

Aje and Nancy to the Akha in Thailand

Aje Kukaewkasem, the young Akha man from Thailand so concerned about understanding my fast-talking English, proved to be an exceptional student and quickly a favorite to the teachers and fellow students. While he attended RMBI, he translated the Psalms into the Akha language. And he earned A's in the coursework. He and his wife, Nancy, returned to Thailand and established the Akha Foundation, which houses 100 orphans, and a Bible school which trains 200-plus students a year. They've planted 23 churches in the mountains and translated the New Testament, Psalms and Proverbs into Akha. They also run a missions compound and reach out to China,

Cambodia, Laos, and Burma. Aje has authored at least 12 books and teaches for Haggai Institute, a well-known leadership training school based in Singapore. One of his latest projects was a huge one: leading a team to translate the entire New Testament into Akha!

He's a modern-day Apostle who loves one wife (which is huge for the people he leads) and has produced two great sons in the faith. He's also the first Akha to earn a PhD.

Can you tell I'm proud of Aje? He has become a dear son in the faith, and he's inspired me with his insatiable desire to learn and study. I've learned much from him on how to minister to the Akha and Thai people, which he does so unselfishly. It's been thrilling for more than two decades to watch and be a part of his growth as an apostle. God gifted him with an amazing ministry flow—Aje has truly become a father to the Akha people, whom he loves dearly.

> See Nancy's story in
> PART TWO: More Stories
> "The Dean as a Mentor and Father."

I enjoy traveling to Thailand every year to spend time with Aje and Nancy and their two boys. Nancy is a great lady of the faith and beloved mother to the Akha people. These two have literally changed the culture of the Akha people group.

CHAPTER 18
Missions Adventures While at RMBI

We walked into a half moon-shaped worship center in southern Africa to a thunderously loud, dancing and singing chaos of 500 people adorned in colorful clothes. The wooden seats couldn't hold their explosive love for the Lord.

What an easy crowd to minister to! I began to preach. One coat flew up in the air. I said some more. Then another jacket went sailing. Then another. They began to get stuck in the rafters. The people were flamboyantly registering their Amens! with their colorful clothes. I'd never experienced such manner of worship to the Lord. A lot of coats and jackets hung from the rafters! I'm sure it entertained the angels and proved quite an experience for the 24 other Americans I'd brought on this trip.

Earlier, around four or five years after our first RMBI class, the desire to take students in RMBI on a missions trip to another nation had begun to stir in me. This would move classroom instruction from theoretical to real life, something I loved to do. Through an FBC missionary connection in Zimbabwe, Africa, we planned this trip. Fifteen students raised their own support along with 10 adults, and it lasted 15 days.

I directed the students to preach every night. After a few nights, some came to me begging, "We're tired! Can't we take a day off?" *Of course not!*

While I preached one night with the pastor interpreting for his congregation, I heard the Holy Spirit whisper that Lana and I should pay his way to Israel. I spoke it out loud. The pastor stopped interpreting and looked at me, surprised. He was totally speechless.

We did get an opportunity to send him to Israel, a blessing for all of us.

"Ask of Me, and I Will Give You the Nations"

Around the year 2000, after the RMBI student trip to Zimbawbe, a person I'd invited to speak in our chapel prophesied over me: "You will be going to the nations. Not just your students and others. But you, too."

I pondered that in my heart. When the Lord saved me in 1968 in Indiana, I'd found a verse in the Bible that became very special to me: Psalm 2:8. "Ask of Me, and I will give you the nations." I prayed that prayer for decades.

Now, God was laying more runways at RMBI with the students for future outreach that would provide more takeoff points to other nations.

First Trip to Pakistan—Could We Start a Bible School?

Back up a bit, before our African trip. The seed of desire from Psalm 2:8 began to germinate in an unexpected way.

At the end of one day, after teaching in RMBI (which was housed in the FBC administration building), I opened the door and greeted Ruben Mendez, one of the FBC pastors, walking toward me.

"I'm getting ready to go to Pakistan," he said. Pray for me." He flashed me his characteristic enthusiastic smile.

"Pakistan?" I repeated.

"Yeah!"

The Holy Spirit spoke to me. *Go with him!*

"Ruben! I'm going with you!"

"Ohhhhh, Pastor Russ. Really?"

I had no money. I had no time. I was running the school. And Lana …

"Sunday I'm having dinner with a man who used to live in Pakistan," Ruben said. "I want you to meet him."

I joined them for dinner and met Muhab Sabre from a village there. He told an amazing story—of how Pakistanis had burned 1,200 homes, and he barely escaped with his life. But he actually videotaped some of the destruction to show later. His friends warned, "You can't stay here! The men who terrorized the village are after you!"

The Pakistani officials warned, "If you come back here, we'll kill you on sight."

Muhab asked for passports to America at the US Embassy.

"No, we can't give you passports," they told him.

So, he and his wife fasted and prayed three days. Officials came back and said, "We'll give you passports." Two days later, a man gave $1,700 for his family to come to America.

That night at dinner, Muhab pleaded for me to go to his village and start a Bible school. He had a kind of makeshift school but knew they'd kill him if he returned.

His Christian friends had stayed in the village, even though other Pakistanis burned it. The international outcry—because they'd also killed people and raped women—was so loud that the government rebuilt the 1200 homes in the village.

So I flew to Muhab's village with Ruben and Susan Mendez to observe and determine if we could start a Bible college there.

Where could we start the school? Did they really want one?

Miraculous Healing of a Boy's Liver

One day, as Ruben and I watched young Pakistani kids playing, we saw one little boy about 8 or 10 standing on the sidelines like a zombie with a glazed look on his face. No movements, just there. We found out he suffered from a severe liver disease, and the doctors couldn't do anything for him—they didn't give him any hope of surviving.

Great compassion filled my heart. "Ruben, let's pray for this boy!"

We did.

A week later, we saw the boy running with his friends, laughing and playing! His parents took him back to the doctor who said, "There's now nothing wrong with your liver." The Lord had miraculously healed him.

Ruben's wife, Susan, got extremely sick in the village. As we prayed and prayed for her, the Lord protected her from death as she lay in a hospital. We cut our trip short at two weeks to fly her safely back to the US, where she healed. Sometimes God heals in different ways.

Healing Among the Muslims in Pakistan—and a Bible School!

The next year, Dave Wurtsbaugh and I boarded a plane and headed overseas to the Pakistan village. That's when we started the Bible school Muhab Sabre

The Pakistani Massage To Die for

Told by Russ Frase

Tired Traveler

I'd traveled for more than 30 hours to Pakistan. The last leg was an 8-hour train ride. Upon arriving, I sat on my luggage, very tired, while a roomful of eyes stared at this white-haired, white-skinned American. My watch showed after 9:00 p.m. their time. And all I could think of was dropping into a bed and falling asleep.

I saw my driver coming toward me as he wove his way through the masses of people in the station, and then he led me to an overcrowded van.

"You're preaching tonight," he said, matter-of-factly.

TONIGHT? The last thing I wanted to hear.

The van coughed to our stop at the crusade site at 9:30 p.m., where I folded out of the vehicle, too exhausted to move very fast.

"Stay back there," someone said as I stood at the back entrance while a group of young girls prepared to toss rose petals and welcome me with a song. The irony of it. I know they meant well, but all I wanted to do was rest my tired body. I leaned against the wall and let out a huge sigh.

Somehow I made it through my message and prayed for

continued...

had begged us to start. We used materials Muhab gave us, some courses already mapped out.

Word got out that we were coming: "the white missionaries from America." Two Muslim men walked 23 miles so we could pray for healing for them. No light shone in their dark and lifeless eyes, and they showed no emotion. Dave and I prayed for healing for them. Then, through a translator, we told them about Jesus the Savior. Something clicked and their eyes brightened, like someone had turned on a light. Smiling, they turned away, as though their long journey on foot was worthwhile.

The Christian Pakistanis in that village warmed our hearts with their cordial, generous hospitality. As we entered a Christian church in the village, little girls joyfully met us with baskets of rose petals. They showered us with the sweet, fragrant flowers as they sang "Welcome, welcome, welcome to our house!"

Miraculous Healing from Five Tumors

Not quite prepared for what the first day of school held, I carefully chose my steps as Dave and I climbed a cluttered stairway outside on the wall of a stone building. *I hope these steps don't fall apart before we make it to the top.*

On the second floor, I peered into a dark room with several wooden slabs without backs. Students filled them, eagerly waiting for us to teach them. The hunger in their eyes cheered my heart. *They really want this new school!*

A couple of adults snuck into the class. Young girls wore scarves, their bright eyes peering from the folded cloth.

We handed out Big Chief writing pads and pens to them, which they juggled on their laps. Raw faith and belief filled the air as they smiled and talked quietly to one another.

My champion dear friend Dave softly prayed for me and backed me up.

Our subject? The Holy Spirit. Our teacher? The Holy Spirit. He was about to teach about Himself in a way that I wouldn't have conceived. In a culture thousands of miles from the US. In a country where I didn't know the language and depended on an interpreter.

But I made myself available to do His bidding. The runway of availability is probably the most important runway of our hearts we can open to the Lord.

Just before I opened my mouth, the Pakistani interpreter said, "One of

many people—until almost midnight.

By then I felt like a zombie.

The Massage

My hosts took me to an enclave of a home behind a wall and into a small room where "rubber chicken" bubbled in a broth.

"Here, let us show you to your room."

I fell down on a hammock-like woven mat. By now, every muscle in my body ached, and I longed for sleep. I half-closed my eyes, and in the haze saw a brown-skinned pastor standing in the doorway. He looked at me with great compassion as a warm smile slid across his face.

"You like a Pakistani massage?" he asked.

There is a God in heaven—and He likes me! I thought as my muscles pressing into the mat screamed at me. *Ahhh, after all I've been through. This will make it all worthwhile.*

I turned on my stomach, and he worked his fingers into my tense muscles. Harder and harder. Deep into the muscles. Where pain released.

I moaned. I cried. It hurt so bad!

"You like?" he asked.

"Yes," I lied.

He dug deeper and harder.

When he got tired, another pastor moved in and took over. *Pain!*

Then, when I thought I'd get a break, a third pastor took over.

continued...

Ten days ... 10 days in front of me.

Sharing with a Friend in Need

"Dave, you haven't had any massage like a Pakistani pastor massage!" I told my dearest friend, Dave Wurtsbaugh, the next year when I brought him to Pakistan with me.

My muscular, construction worker, brick-laying brother liked the idea until a Pakistani pastor jumped on his back. I sat next to him, looking into Dave's face as the massager pressed the heel of his foot on the back of his head.

I rolled off my chair, laughing, as tears flowed out of this man's-man eyes.

"Russ," he said, glaring at me, red-faced. "You wait until I get off this bed."

We laughed about it a lot later.

There's nothing like a Pakistani pastor massage for a tired traveling preacher.

the girls has tumors on her neck, and she wants you to pray for her."

My eyes turned toward a beautiful young lady about 17, with dark long hair, peeking out from a blue scarf loosely wrapped around her head. She shyly stepped forward from her front row seat. Eighteen pairs of eyes darted back and forth from her to me, from me to her. She looked at me expectantly, her brown eyes hopeful.

As she moved closer, I saw on her creamy brown skin five round balls like marbles, protruding from inside her neck.

Fear gripped me. *Where is the "faith-filled man of God" when I need him?* No matter how many times I pray for healing for someone, each time I have to depend on the Lord to show up!

I stepped forward as she waited for me, so young and innocent.

Okay, Holy Spirit! I need Your healing power on this girl.

"Can I touch you?" I asked.

She nodded, brave to let this white man from the West put his hand on her.

I didn't feel any tingling or fire, like I had at times. I didn't shout or scream as I laid my right hand on her neck. The deadly tumors felt smooth and round. I quietly prayed a couple of healing scriptures. And then it happened—*the five bumps disappeared under my fingers.* When I removed my hand, her skin was a smooth as silk.

All. Instantly. Gone.

She put her hand to her neck, her eyes widened, and she smiled.

The children sat on the rough-hewn benches, eyes wide, as their class-mate took her seat again.

The innocent faith of a girl trumped book learning and degrees. So began our first day of Bible school in Pakistan, the lesson on the Holy Spirit, taught by the Holy Spirit.

That experience in Pakistan whetted my appetite for more moving of the Holy Spirit in the nations.

More Missions Trips

I took RMBI students on more missions trips: Mexico, Europe, the Philippines, and Pakistan again, thanks to help from a 80ish-year-old travel agent, Joy Romero, whom Pastor Gerard, missions pastor at FBC, connected me with. I compelled this petite Presbyterian lady to get out of her comfort zone and preach where there was no electricity in the jungles!

I learned a lot from her, too, like some of the details needed in making overseas travel arrangements.

God was up to something. I wasn't sure what but could feel it rumbling in my spirit. A hunger and passion for ministering, teaching the Bible, and discipling people around the world grew stronger as more opportunities to travel arose. These missions trips brought about an increased awareness of the desperate needs in various countries.

Students returned from the trips pouring out testimonies in our chapel services that ignited fire in the class. In a sort of mini-revival, they'd cry about the heartbreaking things they'd seen as they told fellow students stories—and about the God who they saw work many miracles.

It gratified me to encourage each and every student into his or her divine destiny.

It didn't occur to me that these trips could be a harbinger for things to come.

CHAPTER 19
Grounded by Air Traffic Control

" I'm sorry, but the board has decided that unless we can get 50 to 60 more students by January, they'll close Rocky Mountain Bible Institute." Pastor George studied my face with compassion one morning in November 2004.

Fifty or 60 students? That's a tall order! I knew that wouldn't happen. I had thought I'd grow old mentoring and training students—my calling to the grave—in the 2-year program we'd worked so hard to accredit in 1992. During almost one-and-a-half decades, many students had been released into ministry.

But now, this news.

My heart sped up and I looked at my shaking hands.

What would Lana and I do now? Here's where my heart and passion are. What about future students who were hoping to enroll in RMBI? What about those who are not finished with the program? That is the big bummer!

And, I wondered, *where will the financial provision for Lana and me come from now that the school is closing?*

I tried to put it out of my mind, hoping things would turn around and the school would continue. The final word came at the end of January at a financial board meeting.

As we went back and forth, talking about issues, mostly the finances, I asked Pastor George what he wanted to do.

"Close the school."

"Okay."

Pastor George and the elders were very fair with us in providing a six-month severance while we sought the Lord for our next step.

"Give me your résumé," Pastor George said. "I'll put it out everywhere."

I told Lana that night about the board's decision while she ironed clothes. And she started laughing. "Why the hell am I laughing? You just lost your job!"

That broke the tension.

Painful Clearing of the Runways

At first, I couldn't see the Lord in this abrupt change in our direction at all. The closing of RMBI pained me, and I needed to work through that. Another school presented by a staff member was going to take its place, which hurt even more. Information was already being presented to the congregation for this new school.

The last nine years we'd gotten to a place where running RMBI had become like running a fine-tuned machine. Routine. Predictable. The class schedules set. But without feedback I yearned for, a nagging doubt nipped at me—was I *really* doing a good job? It didn't help that for a year prior to RMBI closing, I hadn't gotten an invitation to preach anywhere, and I wasn't preaching at Faith Bible Chapel during this time. No outlet for this preacher man.

One day, while sitting on my back deck in 2003, I cried out to the Lord about the deafening silence and about the feelings of being at a standstill: the routine of running the school, teaching half the classes at RMBI, and not sure the effect I was having.

What's going on here, Lord!

Then, when I'd finished ranting, a familiar Voice sounded in my ear. *I don't care how much you preach. I care more about YOU and your relationship to Me than what you do for Me.*

Not about what I do for Him? Not about my service for Him? But about our intimate connection and partnership—together?

We say that ministry is not our identity, but it can easily become that. Each of us serving the Lord in whatever capacity has to come to that place where we separate *who we are* from *what we do*. That is the lesson my heavenly Father wanted to teach me—and I was learning it in a painful way.

That familiar hunger stirred in my heart. *I want more of You, Lord ... more ...*

I started reading a lot of books on grace. That He did everything for us with the death of His Son on the Christ. That He loves me unconditionally. I sensed Him telling me in my heart, "Hey, whether you do this or not, I love you. Whether you do this or not, you are righteous *in Me, in Christ.* You are accepted in the beloved. You are hidden in Christ. And because of all this, you seek to please Me. Here's the grace. It's not in the law. But in grace I'll keep ya busy."

As I kept reading, kept praying and pondering these things, deeper revelations came to me. The *more* I'd been seeking. I opened the runways of my heart to the new *more* of grace.

As I taught the students by day and sought His wisdom at night, I was confronted by this heart-jolting question: Was I willing to grow at any cost, no matter what blind obedient steps I needed to take?

Internally, I knew I didn't need to please people or receive their applause or affirmation. But digging deeper into my soul, did my beliefs really line up with my actions? Were there times when I wanted to look good? When I wanted to be around the right people? To hear the positive affirmations from people?

We all fight these things—wanting to put ourselves forward. "Impress" the right people. Gear for "success" rather than draw from God's Word and the strength of the Holy Spirit for *His version* of success. We do it either consciously or subconsciously. We've all probably been places where "all the important folk" gather and everyone parades his achievements, each trying to outdo the other. Rather than just go and *be.*

I realized the antidote to this bondage is *to serve others*. And, *It's not about me and what I do. It's about You, Lord.*

As this runway, the runway of affirmation of who I am in Christ, and a greater understanding of His unfathomable grace and forgiveness toward me expanded in my heart, I'd shown up in more places to just serve people.

Grounded

And then, we got the news about RMBI closing. Here came a hard test—of obedience and faithfulness to God.

I'd taught my students it is vital how you exit one situation before you enter another. No matter what happens, it's important to continue in Spirit-led, Spirit-filled, Spirit-indwelt control. We give little attention to this aspect of the Holy Spirit—to giving complete control over to Him, as Paul says in Ephesians 5:18, "And do not be drunk with wine … but be filled with the Spirit." It is this aspect that works maturing graces in our lives, one of the cardinal criteria for the Spirit-filled life to take us beyond the humps of disappointments, discouragements, and distractions.

The Holy Spirit is ready for the downdrafts and turbulence in our lives. All of us have to deal with them. How we handle these matters either determines great success or lesser than what God desires. We all experience them sooner or later: events or circumstances in our lives that position us for success or failure, for moving forward or backward, to complete less than God planned or fulfill our callings.

Now, the test for Lana and me …

In January 2005, after the board told us RMBI would be closing, I knew it was important not to say things we'd regret or would taint the lives of others we came into contact with during a critical transition like this. Even when we didn't understand what was happening, or why, or what our future would look like. There's always the temptation to second-guess the reasons for any decision, especially if it doesn't seem favorable to us. Although I did not agree with the decision to end RMBI, I submitted to leadership's authority.

But it was easier said than done. A raging inferno battled in my mind. I knew the quicker I dealt with it righteously, the better the outcome. It's like the Holy Spirit gave me a *gag* order. I had to clear away any pride or rebellion. If I didn't submit at the heart level, then it wouldn't have been pure and true submission and pleasing to the Lord.

When traveling by plane, a number of times our plane sits unmoving on the tarmac waiting for "okay" from air traffic control. I don't know why it stalls. Maybe a plane in the air supposed to land can't let down its landing gear. Or maybe a sudden microburst of wind has delayed other flights in front of us. Or perhaps a maintenance issue on our own plane has been discovered, or wildlife on the runway needs to be cleared first. I've had to wait three hours in the taxiway—not knowing why—before even getting to the runway.

When we haven't been given the go-ahead by the Air Traffic Controller, we sit. And wait.

And wait.

Lessons from Joshua

In Joshua Chapter 5, Joshua circumcised the young warriors before leading them into the Promised Land. Joshua 5:8 says, "After all the males had been circumcised, they rested in the camp until they were healed."

Another reason why God may not tell us what lies ahead is because we need to heal before we can move forward. It can be dangerous in the larger scheme of God's plans to move forward too soon.

Once the Israelites moved forward, something took place that had not happened in 40 years while they'd been wandering in the wilderness eating daily manna God provided.

> Now the children of Israel camped in Gilgal, and kept the Passover on the fourteenth day of the month at twilight on the plains of Jericho. And they ate of the produce of the land on the day after the Passover, unleavened bread and parched grain, on the very same day. Then the manna ceased on the day after they had eaten the produce of the land ... (Joshua 5:10-12).

For the first time in 40 years, no manna appeared on the day they ate from the harvest of the land—in fact, they never saw manna again.

They were ready to move into the new place, God's promised land.

For me, I needed to clear some obstacles from the runways of my heart in order to receive new graces of spirituality God wanted to give me—many more spiritual realities than just the exciting and thrilling gifts that cause one to *ooh* and *ahhh!* This is the satisfying grace of the Holy Spirit, who, in these experiences, separated in me the works of the flesh and soul and misguided human spirit. Boy, did He have a ton of work to do in my life! He drilled deep into my soul to bring forth new maturity in my character. And, the Holy Spirit cleared obstacles off runways in my life, like unbelief, resentment, and unforgiveness, that would have kept me from taking off into the calling and purpose the Master prepared.

The Holy Spirit: Buffing out the Bumps

The cross is not only the instrument of grace but the circumcision instrument of God, through the death and resurrection of Jesus and execution work of the Holy Spirit—not only growing us up, but maximizing our effectiveness in the kingdom.

When I was 8 years old, I mowed lawns for 25 cents an hour. I was so proud of my first paycheck: $3.75. I ran to the general store and bought that gray, chromium fishing reel I'd salivated over for a year.

One day, after I thought I'd finished mowing a yard, I parked the lawn-mower and walked up the hill to our house. The phone rang.

"Russell," my boss, Leo, said. "You didn't finish the job."

I didn't finish the job? I gave it everything I had! And have the sweat to prove it!

"Come back down. You're not done until you trim the grass around the house, bushes and walks."

Years later, when my son, Rusty, mowed our yard, I'd tell him, "Get back out there and trim the grass. You are not done."

So it is with the Holy Spirit. He is not done until we allow Him to trim the grass and put the finishing touches on our spiritual lives. This is the sometimes silent, searching, deep drilling of the Lord into the recesses of our souls to remove flesh, to remove self, and to add maturity to undone parts of our lives. And to move us forward into yet greater success in ministry.

And, God is always interested in *both parties* in a situation, no matter what the circumstances surrounding it. For my part, not only did I need to submit to authority, but I still needed to clear unforgiveness from the run-ways of my heart. Not pertaining to the actual leadership, but to individuals influential in the decision. Difficult. I thought I'd settled that with one prayer, but realized it was more perfunctory than from the heart. The Holy Spirit, who reveals all things, truly showed me my heart—debris on the runway.

After our last RMBI graduation in May 2005, I sensed I needed to slip into the background, waiting on the taxiway parallel to the runway. Waiting to take off.

Waiting.

Waiting for the Air Traffic Controller to give me the go-ahead.

Positioning the plane for a greater *more* than I'd ever experienced, yet having no clue as to what that was.

CHAPTER 20
Diamonds

In May 2005, I stood on the stage with bittersweet tears as one Rocky Mountain Bible Institute graduate after another crossed in regal-looking robes, taking their diplomas from my hand.

Here they are being released into ministry, but I don't have a ministry. What do you have for us, Lord? What's next? Tomorrow I'll be on a plane to India, but what then?

Lana and I didn't really know what to do, other than what I'd already planned: mission trips and conferences.

After graduation, I joined a team from South Carolina to teach, preach, and minister at crusades in India. The Christian leaders sequestered us in our rooms for security reasons, where we ate spicy french fries and played cards.

Stretched out on my bed, I read in 2 Corinthians, "My grace is sufficient for you, for my strength is made perfect in weakness." I fell asleep and dreamed of a page of scripture and saw in a large font:

Your sufficiency is from God.

I heard these words in the dream: "And you can trust Him."

When I awoke, a peace flooded my soul. Even though our six months' severance would end in December, and Lana and I had *no idea* what we'd do next, I stopped worrying about our future or how the Lord would take care of us. He would.

Several months later while visiting my twin brother, Roy, and his wife Gayle in upstate New York, early one morning I had a vivid dream:

Diamonds fell from heaven, all kinds of them—all sizes, all colors. And I filled my arms up with them in a transparent bushel. I heard the Spirit say, "From now on you will be a diamond catcher."

The "Diamonds" Start Dropping from Heaven

"We've told our Sunday school teacher about you, and we want you to meet him!" Another dear friend we visited in Athens said. "And we want to hear what's going on in your lives these days, too."

After the service, Lana and I went to lunch with our friends, the teacher, his wife, and others at Applebee's.

"So how are things going with your ministry?"

"Well, uh—"

"My son is in college now." He'd turned to the person next to him and started another conversation.

So much for that!

"Oh, by the way," he said turning back to me. "This morning on the way to church, my wife and I decided to give you $25,000. If you will follow us home, we will write you a check."

Lana and I looked at each other. *Did he just say what I thought he said?* Recognition in her eyes told me she'd heard the same thing. Tears sprang from my eyes.

"I've never seen Brother Frase with nothing to say," one of the friends at our table told me later.

Diamonds.

More Provision

A few months later, Lana and I talked about money again, wondering what we'd do. Dear friends and former church members who now lived in Arkansas called us and wanted to give us a few days' vacation at Padre Island before taking us to a missions conference in Louisiana.

Relaxing in a comfortable chair with Lana and our friends in a beautifully furnished suite, I peered through the balcony at the stunning turquoise ocean and listened as the waves gently lapped in the shallow waters. We'd been sharing light conversation and enjoying the view for several minutes.

"How much do you owe on your Toyota?" my friend suddenly asked.

"Hmmm … $9,700 or so."

"I want to send you a check and pay off the car."

Diamonds danced on the water as I took in what he said. *He's paying off my car!*

A month later he called. "How much does Lana owe on her car?"

"$13,000."

"I'm sending you a check."

More diamonds.

A year later, we visited Lana's relatives in Alabama. I walked around the crystal lake in a beautiful park, praying and sensing strongly the presence of the Lord. It was a good season: God providing funds, new ministry doors opening, and our confidence and trust that things were going to work out. My cell phone rang and I pulled it out of my pocket.

"Pastor, I have some gold I am selling, " said the friend who had paid off our cars.

I pushed the phone closer to my ears as he rattled off a figure. I pushed my phone even closer and breathed heavily as I quickened my pace.

"What did you say?" I asked incredulously.

"I want to give the money to you. $54,000."

Diamonds. And more diamonds.

God has provided like this continually since. I've learned to depend on Him more than any other voice I hear, and nobody speaks like Him—there are many voices in the world, but none as safe and secure as His.

He set the stage financially for us to fluidly move from our comfortable place with a salary at Faith Bible Chapel and RMBI to a new place of faith and fruitfulness that we couldn't even have imagined.

He opened up a wide runway of Provision.

"Now to Him who is able to do exceedingly abundantly above all that we ask or think" (Ephesians 3:20).

CHAPTER 21

The Discovery that Birthed Joshua Nations

S o with the provision of the Lord, we looked to our future.

Little did we realize God had set us up for the new move in our lives in other ways. While RMBI continued to train and graduate students before my time as dean ended, several things happened. One Sunday night in January 2001, I was preaching in Life Temple in the Denver area. An energetic Hispanic man, Sam Santos, who pastored a Spanish congregation housed in the church, heard me preach. After my message, he rushed up to me.

"You *must* go to Cuba with me! So much is happening in Cuba. I know a lot of people there." He told me more about it, and it not only piqued my interest, but I felt a familiar excitement rising in my stomach.

"When are you going?" I asked.

"Soon. You *must* go!"

"Okay."

"You say so, but you won't!"

"Yes, I will!"

Sam looked down at the floor and then into my eyes. "All Americans say they will come, but they don't."

"But I will!"

I contacted him some time later. "When are we going?"

He was shocked. Not only that I would go with him but that I put together a team of 10 people. Sam Santos had been going into Cuba for 13 years. He'd held lots of revivals. The pastors and the people loved him there.

The purpose of that first trip was to observe and teach. Flying in from

Miami, we went on a religious visa, which gave us the right to preach and teach all over Cuba.

Religious and Political Climate in Cuba

Although Cuba is a Communist nation, it may surprise many that it was not a closed nation to the gospel. Sam had clued me in, so I was ready for the openness. Considering the history and political restraints of Cuba, it is amazing that we could freely preach in that Communist country. But things had shifted and changed over the years.

Actually, one of our key contacts in the country said there was a lot of religious persecution in the 60s, 70s, and 80s. Many on the island were concerned about attending church. But in 1988, the government gave permission for the first time for small groups of people to meet in houses, and it was established as law. At the same time, Communist countries around the world were collapsing. Germany, Romania, Czechoslovakia, and the Soviet Union. All of them were turning toward capitalism, or becoming free countries.

So, according to our contact, in the 1980s Cuba felt the squeeze of isolation from the world and had no access to things people needed. There was a shortage of almost everything on the island. So people stopped looking to Moscow and they began looking to God. The Holy Spirit was stirring things up! That's when people started attending the churches. That's what the religious leaders called "the first wave of conversions." Their first revival. And with that came a need for materials, for discipleship, for simple ways to teach the people and grow.

It is in that perfectly timed climate the Holy Spirit opened doors for us through Sam Santos to start going into Cuba.

We heard there were about 4,000 churches in the Baptist and Assembly of God denominations (not counting the others) at the time of our first visit in 2001. By that time, churches were told to simply register with the government. Government informants showed up at the church meetings, which were freely held if a church had registered. The informants were just looking for three things:

1. Any mention of "revolution" coming or about starting one.
2. Preachers could not mention anything about Castro.

3. Preachers could not say that Jesus was the answer to the nation of Cuba, because Castro made it clear *he* was the answer.

So when we went into Cuba, we preached about Jesus and all He could do for the oppressed individuals who listened to us, and the government let us do it. They actually considered this in the best interest of the country—uplifting the people and calming them despite their circumstances.

The Cuban People and Their Culture

I enjoyed spending time with the people on the island—they were colorful, lively, and I loved their salsa music!

On almost every street, we saw shirtless men huddled over domino boards on square tables. They smoked long cigars amidst a wasteland of old cars on cement blocks waiting to be repaired. These were likely men who didn't want to, or couldn't, find work for the government.

There were lots of witches and voodoo types walking up and down the streets, which caused us to plead the blood of Jesus over our lives. Though oppressed, the people were nice. They loved us. We'd preach in buildings four stories up with the windows open and Christian music pouring out from them. Our meals included a lot of rice and beans, beans and rice—washed down with warm sodas! We learned quite a bit about the culture on the first trip.

To travel to our meetings, Cubans strapped luggage haphazardly to the top of old Russian cars. We gagged as gas fumes filled the vehicles and we rattled down the street. The pastors held church in homes where small crowds of people gathered under a makeshift lean-to or in a room in a modest house.

On this first trip, I was shocked when, during the worship service in downtown Havana, we saw Israeli dancers. An Israeli Messianic church worshipped there.

"Wow! This is Cuba! There's freedom here!" I remarked to one of our team members.

I also learned a lot about the "protocol anointing" which we followed to the letter. For example, stay submissive to the government and the laws of the land. God honors that. Some preachers don't do that and they get thrown out. Or jailed.

I returned with a team to Cuba one year later in 2002. We traveled more, especially south of the capital, Havana, into the middle of the island. We ministered to hungry people in some of the most modest conditions. We could preach in the homes, but we couldn't witness on the streets. Many people accepted Jesus, and people from the churches discipled them after we left.

The Seven-Mile High Connection
that Dramatically Changed Our Course

In 2003, Lana and I were waiting to fly to Tulsa when the flight attendant said to me, "Mr. Frase, would you mind sitting a few rows back?"

I really didn't want to, but I sensed from the Holy Spirit this was the right thing to do. So I stood and told Lana, "See ya in Tulsa!" then moved to my new seat.

After introducing myself to the couple beside me, I found out that they had been missionaries in Cameroon and Liberia for 28 years. We talked about Africa and RMBI.

Seven miles in the air, Russ Tatro said, "I have a two-year Bible school curriculum with lectures and exams in Spanish that I would like to give to you."

"We don't do anything at RMBI in Spanish." I smiled politely and thanked him for his offer.

I returned home and busied myself in my duties at the Bible institute. About three months later, the Lord sent a missionary from Estonia, an American lady, Sherry Hyntiten, to speak in our chapel service. Afterwards, we were chatting about the nature of missions in Estonia, Russia, and that part of the world. Suddenly, out of the blue, Sherry looked at me and said, "I know a man who has a two-year Spanish Bible curriculum."

"Russ Tatro, right?"

Sherry's eyes widened. "How do you know him?"

"I met him on an airplane, and he offered me this school, also."

She jabbed her fingers at me. "You need this!"

"But, we don't do anything in Spanish at RMBI."

"You need this school, and I am having it sent to you." She left my study that day with an air of finality.

A package arrived in the mail a few days later from Sherry. I opened it, looked at the labor of love Russ Tatro and several African pastors had produced, then turned around and placed it on my credenza.

And forgot all about it.

Two days later, I took a team into Cuba for the third time, to this "little land of great controversy," this Communist-controlled country. It was a few weeks after we returned when I worked in my study and happened to turn around in my chair. I noticed the already-forgotten Spanish curriculum.

"Oh my God, what have I got here?" I flipped through the pages with more intentionality. *What do they speak in Cuba? Spanish!*

Finally, all of heaven had my attention. Bells and whistles sounded, angels were dancing on the heads of needles, and I realized what had occurred. I quickly and excitedly called my Puerto Rican hero.

"Sam, I have a two-year fully developed Bible school in Spanish. Can we use this in Cuba?"

I heard the aged veteran of the faith begin to weep on the other end of the line. "Oh, Brother Russ! I have been praying for 13 years for a Bible school in Cuba."

Heaven's desire met earth's needs for the nation of Cuba. Finally the majesty of God had broken through my thick head and gotten my attention. God had given me a seven-mile-high divine resource for the nation of Cuba.

And, for many other nations, as it turned out.

Sixty-Seven Cents

In 2005, when our team landed on the island again, we met a pastor with a map of the nation of Cuba tacked on his wall and a vision in his heart to reach the whole island with the gospel. We told him about the Bible school.

"Did you know that in the very next room I have printing presses?" he asked.

Oh, my gracious! This man with a vision for reaching Cuba can print our Spanish curriculum? But can we afford it?

"What is the cost to print one book?"

He smoothed his hand over the map as a smile spread slowly across his face. "Let me call my printer in."

After crunching the numbers, he said, "For each book, 67 cents."

I nearly fell over! Only 67 cents for two years' worth of Bible teaching for a school?

One of my team members said quickly, "I will pay for 1,000 books."

"I will pay for another thousand!" said another.

We laughed and nudged one another at the hilarity of God's awesome provision, right there in Cuba.

A third team member piped up. "One thousand from me!"

"I'll take care of the fourth set of 1,000 books!" I said.

And before our eyes a miracle of epic proportions was birthed in modern-day Cuba. The first 4,000 books were printed. From this time on, Joshua Nations began providing Bible curriculum for schools all over Cuba, including great favor in the prisons.

One of our first pastors hauled the printed books all over the island in the back seat of his dilapidated, rusted-out car.

Eight Cuban leaders started schools on the main island and also on the Isla de la Juventud, Island of Youth, just west of Havana. They started them wherever they could get the space: in churches, a living room, a lean-to shed, or on a dirt floor somewhere.

There was no training process in those days. But it took off like wildfire! It was not our doing at all, but the Lord's. The Holy Spirit opened doors and led us, superintending the whole thing. We were just holding on for dear life. Soon, so many schools were opening we were blessed to print 23,000 or more sets of curriculum. This kept our home office and stateside volunteers busy in handling the whole process.

Before we knew it we were conducting graduations in Cuba every January.

The Meanest Man in Havana

They called him the meanest man on the streets of Havana. He burned up police cars, destroyed a lot of property, and masterminded violent crimes. Officials sentenced him to 197 years in prison.

Just two weeks in the tank, he accepted Jesus's offer of salvation. Someone had smuggled in the Joshua Nations curriculum. His anger turned to kindness, and love filled the place in his heart where hate used to reign. Officials reduced his sentence to 96 years, and then further reduced it to 34 years, of which he'd served 13. Prison officials recognized him as a model prisoner and gave him special privileges and responsibilities. Fellow inmates looked to him as their pastor.

The warden gave him the keys to one of their government cars to visit us, unsupervised, during one of our trips to Cuba.

When a man in a green jumpsuit popped in on us before a graduation, we realized who he was. The former "meanest man" in Havana.

"Would you speak to the graduates?"

He did. At the graduation, we also met his wife, who radiated joy. He saw her on a regular basis after he proved his character in prison.

After the ceremony, a handful of us men gathered for Cuban coffee in a cafe to relax and talk. I looked up and saw him—green jumpsuit and all—coming toward us, very animated and eager to speak to us. We were stunned as he stood beside our table talking very fast.

He sat with us and spent more than an hour telling us about the things happening in the prisons: many men coming to salvation, deliverance from demons, healings and miracles.

This news astounded us. Tears filled our eyes as we listened to story after amazing story. And the truth of the grace of God in this one man's life touched me deeply. *And we're part of this story. Unbelievable!*

"Before the warden leaves to go home for the night, he gives me the keys to the room to the prison printing presses," he told us. "All night long I print Joshua Nations curriculum on the Communist printing presses."

Some of the prisoners made me a beautifully carved wooden plaque, I guess in their workshop, while in prison.

In beautifully carved script surrounded by carefully detailed flowers,

"Joshua Nations is known all over the island and greatly respected," a high Cuban government official said recently.

It's mind boggling, the power of the Holy Spirit to speak to us, lead us, and guide us—to give divine appointments, even when we are unaware of what God is doing and we can say, "This has truly been a work of God, and we have simply been available to do his bidding."

Discerning the Voice of God for Guidance

Told by Russ Frase

I've been learning better how to discern God's direction for me and the ministry. I often seek Him for 2–3 hours in the mornings on my back deck under the trees, asking the Holy Spirit to show me what I am to do. My favorite go-to passages for guidance are Proverbs and Psalms. Then, if I'm sensitive enough, listening enough, I will understand what He's showing me to do, where to go, who I'm going to be with—and, when to accept or decline invitations.

As things unfold, I've found the Holy Spirit drops in surprises while meeting with people. I get a general idea ahead of time, but when talking with them, God gives me more information and understanding on what He's given me.

I was scheduled to go to Honduras the first part of November in 2015. This trip was not clicking in my Spirit. I talked to the guy who wanted me to go.

He told me truthfully, "Y'know, we are in transition. Staff changes. It's probably not a good time to come!"

"Oh, good!" I said. "Because I'll tell you what's working with me. I'm supposed to go to Africa, in Rwanda and the Congo, and graduate hundreds of students. But I didn't want to leave you in the lurch, and we had cancelled this several times. If you are good, then, I'm good ... we can look at me coming in 2016."

If it is the Holy Spirit, then it will flow. There's not a catch. Not a red flag. When things aren't coming together, then I know I've planned something I shouldn't have or circumstances are changing.

the plaque looks like a book that reads on the left side [*sic*]:

To: President: Joshua Bible
Institute USA
Dr. Russ Frase
The: Cuba
God
Bless
You

And on the right side:

"You sympathized with those in prison and joyfully accepted the cousiscation [sic] of your property because you knew that you yourselves had better and lasting possessious [sic]."
Hebrews 10:34
Mt. 25:39–40

We'd smuggled the curriculum behind bars at first, and then it became accepted and even some of the guards eagerly studied it and graduated from our small prison schools. Receiving that plaque made by the Cuban prisoners' own hands humbled me and made me grateful that I'd obeyed the Lord—and finally accepted the Spanish curriculum Russ Tatro offered me on that life-changing flight.

CHAPTER 22
Joshua Nations
Expands on Many Runways

Rocky Mountain Bible Institute closed in 2005, and we officially launched Joshua Nations in 2007. The day after the last RMBI graduation, questions filled my mind: *What are Lana and I going to do with our lives? Are we going to be supported? What does God want from us now? What direction should we go?* We pondered and prayed, and people asked us the same question, "What are you going to do?"

And the Lord assured me while in India, *My grace is sufficient.* That gave me peace, and we took one step at a time forward as we felt the Lord leading. I sensed our calling would probably be missions and going to the nations in some context, though I had no idea when or how or even if this was it.

Flying over the Runways in LA

In 2006, the Lord gave me a strong impression at the airport in Los Angeles as we flew in from an international trip—stated in the preface of this book and that gave me the title for the book. As I saw the layout of runways below, the Holy Spirit spoke to me.

There are many runways down there to receive airplanes from all over the world. Without those runways planes could not land—planes carrying important cargo.

It's the same with your heart. It is full of runways on which I desire to land My spiritual realities. I have so much for you, but if you don't allow Me access to the runways of your heart—arteries for the vital life flow of My Spirit—I cannot fulfill my purposes, plans, and pleasures in your life.

You must give Me complete runway access.

If you do, you'll be amazed at the treasures I want to give you—the precious cargo I want to deliver to you. The wings of the Holy Spirit will fly the spiritual realities of the Father and Jesus into your heart. Surrender completely to Me and watch what we can do together.

Partnerships

The Lord gave us impetus for growth and one of our most significant partnerships at the beginning was with Global Advance, headquartered in Rockwall, Texas. Soon after in 2005, we discovered the printing press in a back room in Cuba and began to print books and opened 175 schools (without the strategic plan developed yet for Bible Training Centers). Global Advance leaders heard about what God was doing in Cuba. In 2006 (after RMBI closed and after the "Diamonds" dream when God showed me He would provide in the next chapter of our journey), Global Advance founder Dr. David Shibley and International Director Dale Witt invited me to come to Dallas to tell them about what was happening in Cuba.

"Will you train our leaders to start schools with your curriculum?" Dr. Shibley asked.

Global Advance had many connections in countries all over the world. We provided a valuable piece for their team, so the partnership proved symbiotic. They'd come in the front door with the Frontline Shepherd's Conference in various nations. Then, after they left, Joshua Nations would come in through the back door and continue training.

Okay, so at least part of our mission is taking this curriculum to the nations, I thought.

I accepted invitations to help with Global Advance Frontline Shepherd's Conferences with a small team of leaders from across the nation. I soon found myself in a mentoring relationship with Dale Witt, who taught me how to operate an international missions conference—from dealing with budgets to how to work with international leaders and how to put together a team of people to conduct strategic sessions of leadership training. This proved valuable for the future. God prepares us for where He's taking us. Even though I didn't know where we were going, He led us each step of the way.

We initially named our 501-c3 "Joshua Ministries." Stan Sinclair, the creative, multitalented worship leader at FBC, offered to talk with me about our branding and logo.

We met on a Thursday in the church atrium for lunch. "You want to reach out to the *nations*, don't you?" he asked.

I nodded.

"Then, shouldn't you have 'Nations' in your name, rather than just 'Ministries'?"

So, Stan created the first Joshua Nations logo for us.

Pastor Roger Gerard, missions pastor for FBC, told our congregation that Lana and I were transitioning to missions work in the nations.

Things seemed to be falling into place for our new direction. I'd learned a lot for RMBI on accreditation at the conference in Tulsa and while traveling as national accrediting chairman for the International Christian Accreditation Association (ICAA). And, seeing the hunger in Cuba and a zeal for starting Bible schools with curriculum from Russ Tatro's Living Waters ministry, strategies for how Joshua Nations would operate started taking shape.

We partnered with other organizations, including International Ministers Alliance (IMA), a consortium of 1100 pastors; World Missions Evangelism (WME); and Great Commission Fellowship (GCF). They support us in several ways at this time of publication, including financially and with networking connections in the various nations. They also provide more opportunities for us to start Bible Training Centers and train leaders how to plant churches, the core of what Joshua Nations offers.

They've proven to be friends of mine for many years, and I am grateful for these organizations.

Creation of the Strategic Plan for Leadership Training

Yet a key component of the foundation of Joshua Nations was still missing, and we soon discovered Kristina Vickery held that piece. She returned to the US after serving two years in Jerusalem (2005–2006) as International Administrative Director for Bridges for Peace. She shared with me a dream the Lord gave her, while in Jerusalem, of coming alongside me and helping to produce diplomas.

"Whatever that means," she said.

We met and she showed me a PowerPoint presentation the Lord had inspired her to create the previous day: a suggested national structure for whomever He'd send to any nation.

That initial structure formed the basis for what Kristina created for us the next few months. (See "Creation of the Joshua Nations Strategic Plan" sidebar.) She became a valuable coach and mentor to Lana and me, and she expertly wrote the initial Vision & Strategic Plan we used to train our trainers for setting up Bible Training Centers. (That plan has evolved through the years as new insights in working with the nations have come.)

Using the key components of Vision, Mission, Goals, Strategies, Tactics, Assessment, and Measurement, this plan spelled out how trained Joshua Nations representatives could equip pastors, leaders, and others to set up simple and self-sustaining Bible Training Centers in churches, homes, schools in their nations. We'd help with some of the initial needs, such as printing and providing the curriculum for them, but with Kristina's help, we have mapped out a way for them to continue the centers with their own resources, an important strategy in order for us to reach more and more countries and people groups.

Sharing the Vision with Prospective Reps

The vision the Lord gave me for teaching the nations the Word of God burned in my heart, and I knew I needed help for such a huge vision. I invited people to an all-day meeting in Arvada, Colorado, in Spring 2007, to share this strategic plan—those who'd been on various trips with us or who ministered in various countries. Some were RMBI graduates.

Kristina and I presented the plan to 18–20 people to see what kind of interest we could drum up. I shared this about Joshua Nations:

> **Our Vision:** To disciple the nations.
>
> **Our Mission:** That unbelievers become believers, believers become disciples, disciples become leaders, leaders become fathers, fathers become leaders of leaders.
>
> **Our Goals:** To establish Bible Training Centers, to disciple, to equip, to reproduce, to encourage, to redeem, to provide, to exemplify, to become.
>
> **Our Strategies:** Discipleship, leadership and stewardship.

A petite, blond widow named Bobbie Stratman attended that meeting in Arvada.

After class, I went around to each person to ask what they thought about the day. When I reached Bobbie, sitting on the front row, tears filled her eyes, and she looked like she wanted to talk but couldn't at first.

"I've gone to China to smuggle in Bibles and training materials since 1995, and this is what China is missing. We share Jesus, but there's no follow-up discipleship."

"So, what do you think?" I asked.

"I feel God is showing me today this is what I'll do."

I made Bobbie the global team lead for Joshua Nations for China (and later, Southeast Asia) that day.

Now, I sensed the plan from the Lord unfolding: that God would provide representatives, in addition to me, who would go to various countries to train leaders on this strategic plan for setting up BTCs.

In May 2018, this 71-year-old passion-filled grandma celebrated her 10th anniversary with Joshua Nations. She has her own non profit, Empowering Grace, International, and has worked tirelessly and sacrificially to train more than 4,000

Creation of the Strategic Plan, Leadership Training to Start BTCs

By Kristina Vickery
007 Jesus Agent

Initial Meeting with Pastor Russ

While in Israel serving as international administrative director for Bridges for Peace, I had several dreams at night of what I would be doing while stateside, one of which, was helping Pastor Russ create and copy diplomas for multiple recipients.

I met with Pastor Russ in 2006 to discuss some things on my heart: after many weeks of prayer, a presentation flowed from me as a suggested national structure for whomever God would send to Bulgaria or any nation for that matter. He very unpresumably, as not to assume any rights or privileges, offered to buy the structure. It kind of surprised me, but I was like "Oh no, no—it's kingdom, you're welcome to it—go with it, it's yours!" That initial PowerPoint presentation formed the scaffolding for the global structure that I created in the months to come. It is not a "rocket science" structure—it is a basic, pragmatic approach to help leaders create an infrastructure to facilitate and supply resources, both relational and functional.

Pastor Russ invited me to begin working with he and Lana as they continued...

noodled out the Joshua Nations innards.

"We Need That Plan— Yesterday!"

But then we faced a game changer, really unbeknownst to both of us. Pastor Russ was scheduled to meet with some of his buddies in Dallas with Global Advance, and they had penciled in Pastor Russ to train several of their leaders how to start Bible Training Centers. *The only problem was that we did not have a Leadership Training Program.* Pastor Russ would teach from his notes, but we had no formal approach. The era of needing it yesterday began ...

That propelled us to action! I wrote the Leaders Training Tract on Strategic Planning and a Financial Kit, to train, equip, and empower leaders in their ministries without being dependent on outside funding. The tool to teach leaders how to prepare, plan, and manage their future growth, again, not rocket science, just basic and practical information—but necessary intel to win the game.

The Holy Spirit Brings It All Together with Many Resources

From that time on, Pastor Russ and I met regularly. And, it should be said, we were all simple and sincere people trying to give our best for God's big, very big vision which He'd entrusted to Pastor Russ!

We then worked on "packaging" the program by designing

continued...

leaders to start BTCs. As of the end of 2017, we had printed 55,000 books for students she influenced. I've been privileged to fly to these countries to graduate students and encourage and minister alongside Bobbie not only in China, but also two other countries—Thailand and Burma.

See PART TWO:
More Stories
"Russ's Prophetic Words Propelled Me into Destiny."

Jack Gaudin, an RMBI graduate, also attended that meeting, and though he didn't sign on as a rep right away, God planted seeds of interest that grew in his heart.

A few years later he became a rep for Joshua Nations and is a key leader and teacher in the organization. He ministers full time, teaching on healing and deliverance, and trains leaders to start BTCs.

The hearts of others were touched by the possibilities.

Humanitarian Projects

Before we'd planted one Joshua Nations Bible Training Center, we began believing God for schools in 10 nations. That seemed like such a daunting vision at the time. Little did we know that by 2010, we'd far surpass that goal.

We also teamed up with Diane Brask of Global Seed Planters to reach out with humanitarian projects in areas of Africa with people she knew, traveling with her and ministering to people with great needs. Joshua Nations bought a tractor that would enable farmers in Africa to grow and harvest crops and brickmaking machines.

And we've added other humanitarian projects, such as water wells, with more partners in Uganda, Mexico, and others.

Oral Bible Training

One of Diane's greatest passions is to reach those who cannot read or write (even in their own languages) around the world. This was a completely new concept to me—a school without books? But then Diane posed the question, "What if I can't read? Does that mean I can't go to Bible school?"

I listened carefully as Diane shared alarming statistics about oral learners.

"Almost 7 out of 10 people in the world are either illiterate or pre-

a branding sleeve to pour all the materials into, and before the ink was dry, nation after nation was exploding! At the same time, we designed a website that could accommodate growth, function as an online resource center, and receive funding for people wanting to partner with JN. And just like in my dreams a couple of years earlier, we created diplomas ready for print, just days before some of these students were graduating. Pastor Russ began traveling all over the world graduating students, training leaders, and opening nations—his now normal lifestyle!

God provided all kinds of people to work with us, some fading out of the process and some fading in with larger roles. It was a very fluid and fluctuating time. Pastor Russ welcomes all to the table, and there were a lot of folks helping both logistically and relationally—proofreading, typing, printing, developing the website structure and content, writing, communications. All undergirded by intercessory prayer warriors.

And so, missionaries deployed, under the lead of Pastor Russ, to various nations.

As fast as we could make a brick, Pastor Russ was paving roads to the nations!

Jesus destined that I would come alongside Pastor Russ, an elder and true father in the faith, to create a Leadership Training track that was a direct download from the Lord's heart, as well as create a global administrative

continued...

infrastructure that would naturally expand as the ministry expanded. It was an awesome time for me, and I have so enjoyed watching Joshua Nations flourish!

You can download that plan for free at joshuanations.org/training-video and click on the "English Start-up Kit in pdf" button.

ferred oral learners," she said. "They can't, don't, or won't read or write. They do not learn by our traditional Western methods of lesson plans, lectures, books, and note taking."

Even though it was outside my comfort zone, I knew Diane was on to something. I knew if Joshua Nations was to equip leaders in all nations, we would need a strategy that would empower illiterate leaders.

Diane had developed a specialized oral curriculum, and she spoke at our October 2015 Joshua Nations banquet to our supporters about this. And in January 2017, she launched a pilot program to train 150 leaders in India—those who were illiterate but who hungered to disciple others and set up schools with the model that students could earn a diploma without being able to read or write but could share the gospel by word-of-mouth.

She calls her program the "Story Revolution." We are so pleased that, riding the tracks of relationships we've built, this new type of education can tap into the 70 percent of the world's oral learning population. And plant a whole new kind of Bible Training Center and give natives tools for training and discipling leaders in a way they can understand.

"As fast as we could make a brick, Pastor Russ was paving roads to the nations!"
—Kristina Vickery

CHAPTER 23

Impact of
Joshua Nations

As new avenues opened to us for Joshua Nations and God's timing and direction became clear, the Holy Spirit not only dropped precious treasures on the runways of my heart as He molded and tested my character and built my faith, but He also dug deep to lay a strong foundation, to create stable runways to take off from, and to prepare the runways for landing all around the world.

Of the 500 students who graduated from Rocky Mountain Bible Institute, we figured approximately 33 percent entered into full-time or part-time international and stateside missions or local church ministry. In the years since RMBI closed, my continuing relationships with many of the students keep me involved in their ministries in the US and around the world. I fuel my "jet" and fill it with resources—books, study materials, financial provision, spiritual and personal encouragement—to take to them on a regular basis while maintaining our relationships, a great joy to me!

Only eternity will register the impact of RMBI and what God has done through those whom He brought into our classrooms. It is my great honor and privilege to work alongside so many incredible servants of the Lord all around the world during the last 26 years. "Faithful" describes all of them. I think the greatest impact of RMBI was on me as a person and a leader. The students taught me so much, and those were most

See PART TWO:
More Stories
"Runways of the RMBI
Graduates to the Nations"

blessed and fruitful years. It is a joy to still be involved in many of their lives and ministries.

Testimonies From Students About The BTCs:

All testimonies from BTCs told by Jack Gaudin, *JN Global Rep* *www.FreeToBeFruitful.com*

I Did Not Have Many Words

"I did not have many words to speak before, but now I have words to speak concerning the Word of God. I was empowered and am grounded in the Word so I can preach now."

What the Holy Spirit Has Accomplished

The impact of Joshua Nations since its beginning in 2007 has been astounding. To think that now, at the time of writing in August 2018, we would have 7,300 schools in 60 nations in 56 languages with 153,200 students and 35,000 graduates! This has truly been the hand of God. The divine appointments and divine connections have thrust us into a worldwide ministry we could have never imagined. The influence of the Bible Training Centers is far beyond our ability to measure. As we take off from runways and soar to new heights, God shows us more and more of Himself and of those around the world He wants to reach.

The Holy Spirit rapidly expanded the reach of the Word of God and discipleship through Joshua Nations Bible Training Centers in a way that no man could have ever done. I am continually amazed at how God moves and how He uses passionate, ordinary people to do so. Through Russ Tatro the Lord entrusted me with the curriculum (in several languages) that became the basis for our BTCs, so I am well aware that I am merely a vessel of the Lord, passing something along. I couldn't be more grateful to be part of what He's doing in the earth in these end times, as the Holy Spirit wildfire of teaching and discipling in biblical truth spreads across the nations.

We Equip, Disciple, and Provide Resources

We equip and empower leaders to plant BTCs and churches throughout the world. We also encourage them to fulfill their office gifts of Apostle, Prophet, Evangelist, and Pastor/Teacher (Ephesians 4:11–14).

We have trained thousands of pastors and evangelists to win multitudes to Christ and then disciple them into servants of the Lord. And starting BTCs in countries around the world has also created a large labor force for local churches, a huge help for them.

The residual impact of Joshua Nations and its ability to transform lives wherever it goes will continue far into the generations to come. The empowering of nationals is not only biblical, but also it is very strategic.

Our strong intentional focus and strategic action is why we are so fruitful in the nations.

We also provide resources for computers, motorbikes, and books, which has given much-needed help to current and next generation leaders. The massive printing of more than 300,000 sets of curriculum, 15,000 Holy Spirit manuals, and other materials fuels the faith of graduates and pastors in many leadership conferences.

Reports come in often of more schools being started, of transforming testimonies of God's grace and goodness through the effectiveness of JN in so many places. We are not only giving them fish to eat, but we also are teaching them how to fish and trust God for all they need, which is huge. The equipping and empowering of nationals allows the work of Joshua Nations to continue on many fronts. Our desire is to leave a lot of low-hanging fruit on trees for others to harvest in the years to come.

As mentioned previously, by collaborating with other ministries, such as Diane Brask of Seed Planters International, we have impacted people around the world by channeling funds to improve lifestyle through humanitarian and marketplace ministries, and

TESTIMONY

My Life Has Now Changed

"I did not have knowledge of the Bible before, but my life has now changed. I found out I have administration and leadership gifts, and I can lead people now. And zeal for the lost became very much."

by partnering to drill water wells and provide brickmaking machines. A tractor in Uganda has enabled the growing and harvesting of crops while creating a huge economic benefit to the locals. The people now build churches and pastors' homes, and many have an income they didn't have before.

I have written and produced a Holy Spirit manual (*The Holy Spirit: The Person, Work and Ministry of the Holy Spirit,* available from Joshua Nations and on Amazon), which has gained traction in several nations and in America. This manual has been translated into a dozen or so languages, and we have placed over 10,000 copies so far in the hands of key leaders in Cuba.

People wonder how these statistics could be so high. How do we know these statistics are accurate? It is hard for us to believe ourselves. Because of our structure involving our national and international reps and global reach of the partnerships, we are able to easily find and train leaders how to set up Bible Training Centers and plant churches in many nations. We developed a reporting process and diligently track down the numbers from national and regional leaders and keep a running total each month. We diligently search these out through Skype, email, visiting the nations, and phone calls.

Impact of Graduating on Students around the World

I have not yet seen a graduate who was not overcome with the moment when they could get their hands on that Joshua Nations diploma. It seems like such a small thing to us in the US. But for those who have completed limited education—even those who have gone further—this is the moment of a lifetime for them. How it lifts graduates to a level they never thought they could achieve!

Every graduation is a big deal to students and to me.

As our bus pulls up to the venue, our boat crosses the water, our van rumbles over trenches or bounces over boulder-size holes in the roads, my heart speeds up with excitement to see the proud graduates waiting for us to come, cheering us on.

For me it is the accumulation of 50 years of education, learning, and experience all packed into those moments of euphoric joy. It is the fulfillment of the Great Commission and is dear to the heart of Jesus. I realize I am paying back to Him for making me so wealthy in the riches that money cannot buy. It is far greater than being a billionaire many times over.

> ## TESTIMONY
>
> ### I'm No Longer Discouraged
>
> "The Bible school equipped me so I'm no longer discouraged for lack of knowledge of the Word of God to minister."

Prisoners Set Free with Truth

"Who are they?" I asked my Cuban translator after handing diplomas to a group of ladies.

"They've come to receive diplomas for their husbands, who are in prison. The men attended the Joshua Nations classes there."

As one wife took the diploma from my hand, she looked at me with a million thanks in her eyes. I'll never forget that look of deep gratitude. Tears welled up as I realized the sacrifices and impact to these families who were given a simple discipleship tool.

Graduates came from eight different prisons. That humbled our team members and touched their hearts.

Only 25 Robes

We conducted ten whirlwind graduations throughout Cuba on one early trip. During our first graduation stop in Havana, there were 173 graduates and only 25 robes. One group would come forward, each receive his or her diploma, wait for pictures, then march to the back.

They'd take their robes off and put them on the next set of graduates.

Cuba: 673 Graduates in a Room for 300

On one trip to Cuba, 673 graduates sardined into a room that should hold 300 at the most.

After that ceremony everybody wanted pictures of me, Lana, or a team member. Graduates were so excited they pushed and shoved in the jam-packed room, getting in front of each other to get to the team. It was sheer pandemonium! As we posed for pictures, I noticed a little old man fighting his way to the front. I'd see his head bobbing above the crowd; then it would disappear, reappear, disappear as he worked his way to the front. After he got on the stage, he took my face in his hands and cried, "I have been waiting to see the man who brought us the book!" Well, that moment has blessed me these 11 years. Always to God be the glory!

I realized that this was not only about these graduates, but all of the 28 churches participating and all the leaders, denominational leaders, families, and friends. This was a moment that any pastor or leader would want to be a part of. This was one of the greatest moments of my 50 years in ministry. I thanked the good Lord for allowing me to be a part of this. I vowed I would take Joshua Nations everywhere we could, to make disciples, which is the heartbeat of Jesus. I realized all of these graduates were the ones Jesus died for. My runway of blessing was overflowing.

By 2018, we'd graduated more than 19,000 students on this tiny island. What a joy to pray over them and release them into the Lord's harvest!

TESTIMONY

Now I Know God Has A Plan For My Life

"When I was first born again, I didn't know that I should do any more than to just go to church. But now I know God has a plan for my life, and I have been inspired to open a fellowship in my community."

The Man with the Official Paper

Another Cuban graduation story:

I stood before a crowd, holding the microphone, ready to talk at a graduation.

A man came walking briskly up the aisle waving a sheet of paper. He wanted to speak to the crowd.

Oh, God. We're outta here! Here it comes—a government official, closing us down!

Just the night before, a pastor was afraid to hold the ceremony at his church, and they quickly changed the location to another church in Havana. Somehow they secretly got the word out to those involved—or so we thought. But then, this man had come in off the streets and through the open back door.

I whispered to our operations leader in Cuba, Donato, "What should we do?"

"You'd better let him speak," Donato said.

I was scared. *It's a government guy, and he's going to throw us out of there, and we can't finish the graduation.*

Turns out, this was a father who'd prayed for his son who'd been in prison for many years. His heart ached for a sign from God that his son had come to know the Lord or come back to the Lord.

TESTIMONY

I Didn't Understand The Word Of God

"I was a pastor's wife and Christian for 23 years, but I didn't understand the Word of God. I learned and grew more going through the first year of the Joshua Nations Bible school than I had in all of my 23 years of being born again. It has equipped me to minister the Word of God, and I now encourage all pastor's wives to go through the school."

"This is my sign!" He exclaimed, waving the paper in front of the crowd. A telegram from the prison—which is *unheard* of. It was from the son saying he was graduating that day at the Joshua Nations graduation. Would his dad get his diploma for him?

Somehow, by a miracle, the father found out where the *new* location of the graduation was—only the Holy Spirit could have pulled that off!

This grateful father had dropped everything to pick up his prodigal son's Bible school certificate.

Each Different but Powerful

Every graduation is different and soul shaking to me. Teams who go with us are transformed by what they see, feel, and experience. Sometimes we graduate only 50 or so, and at other times it's several hundred.

And, oh those Africans! Many times because of transportation issues, we show up 2 to 3 hours late, and they have been singing and waiting for us to come.

They sing, dance their way up the aisle, hug, and let out a shrill yell, and the party is on! Sometimes we march in their parades through their towns, parades not for the faint. They want us to march with them 30 minutes to an hour up and down dusty roads that are full of deep potholes. But when we do, we are surrounded by such joyous celebration!

I think the best graduations are the ones poorly managed, conducted in churches with dirt floors, with the sun beaming through the bamboo walls. Or on the islands of Lake Victoria (the world's largest tropical lake, located in Africa, almost 27,000 square miles) where the buildings are dilapidated wooden boards and look like they are about to fall over. These graduations are always followed by eating humble food from boiling pots of rice and some type of meat.

My heart warmed watching the blind man (tutored in the school by another student) peck his cane down the aisle to get his diploma. I never tire of seeing an old man or elderly momma walk the aisle, shouting for joy. Or a whole family graduating together.

And the ones that grab my heart over and over are the young teenagers eager and excited to receive their reward for two years of study.

Sometimes we graduate folks in comfortable surroundings, like beautiful church buildings with air-conditioning. Every now and then the pews are even padded! Sometimes the floors are marble. But sometimes it's brutal driving through the jungles or deserts to a makeshift building to speak to the graduates there and hand out diplomas.

Greg Johnsen, Steve Owings, Jack Gaudin, and I ministered and spoke at nine graduations in Sierre Leone, Africa, with Momma Peggy Cummings, in difficult conditions. We drove over bone-jarring and deep-rutted roads, slept on old couches and uncomfortable beds. We traveled from place to place with little food, sleep deprived, fighting off mosquitos, helping and praying for bleeding travelers when a bus overturned, and fixing blown-out tires. But it amazed me how the good news is multiplying deep in the jungle thanks to Peggy's love and steadfastness.

Deeply embedded in my mind is one of those graduations conducted on the Island of Youth off the coast of Havana. We flew to the Island of Youth not knowing how many would graduate. I discovered they had students from all over the island. As they were marching up the aisle to get their diplomas, I noticed an old lady with them. The closer she got to me she was saying, "Don't stop coming! Don't stop coming to Cuba!" And she got closer and closer, and I reached out and embraced her. I was crying by then. Such appreciation.

Almost wherever we go, students are excited—as though they are graduating from Harvard with a PhD. Every time we get off our bus, many times way out in the sugarcane fields, and walk into the churches, the people are singing, dancing, reaching out to touch us with eyes full of joy. I feel like the Apostle Paul who couldn't describe his visit to the third heaven. Sometimes we conduct three graduations in a day. And minister late into the evening, then drive 30 minutes to an hour to our hotel. I plop down in my bus seat, sweat-drenched, bones screaming, so happy and satisfied I can't stand it, wondering how and why God uses the likes of me to touch the world in such a way.

What Sam Started with One Book
Told by John Wandera
Native Regional Leader of BTCs in Uganda, Kenya and the Congo

"Hey! What can we do? I'm using one book to train 50 leaders!" Sam had started training pastors and leaders in Uganda, Africa. He didn't make copies because he couldn't afford it.

I'd taken Sam under my wing shortly after I started teaching people the Joshua Nations curriculum in Uganda in 2013, training him. With his life transformed by the gospel and excited to help other people who never had a chance to study the Word of God, Sam had called together leaders and pastors, but now realized how hard it was with only *one book*.

I communicated the need to Pastor Russ. The curriculum got translated into his dialect (we have 54 in Uganda), as well as four other dialects, and into the hands of those who needed the materials.

As of late 2016, single-handedly, Sam started more than six training centers, each with at least 25 students per semester.

It's amazing what you can do with just one book in Africa!

Graduations for Denver Inmates

Recently, Lana and I had the opportunity to join with Carl and Lani Rogers as 41 graduates crossed the stage at the El Shaddai Church in Denver, Colorado. This is a small portion of what the on-fire pastor Empress Lugo's very fruitful involvement as a Joshua Nations rep does. She also teaches the curriculum at the Denver Reception and Diagnostic Center along with Carl, and they have had amazing influence on the inmates there. It is a temporary intake and classification facility, and many come and go from there each year.

Hundreds have been exposed to biblical principles through the Joshua Nations curriculum, and we have graduated 476 as of the spring of 2018.

The Impact Is Worth the Work

I think how blessed I am! How marvelous are the works of the Lord! The showcase in heaven is truly thousands of miles long. Sometimes my heart can barely take it in. I had no idea 50 years ago when I said yes to preach my first message what was in store for me. When I hear the multitude of testimonies of those who have completed their studies, of the transformed lives of those released into ministry, I bow my heart to heaven and give God all the glory. This is His doing from start to finish! The Alpha and Omega and all that is in between.

For this reason with joy (well, most of the time) we put up with the gut bugs, the cold showers, the dirty rooms, the hard beds, the bugs on the sheets, the parasites, the food, the heat, the uncomfortable transportation, the long flights, the raising of funds—what a joy, all for Jesus. These are all minor inconveniences compared to those who have gone before us; it is not a sacrifice or suffering but an honor to serve our King.

I resonate with the Queen of Sheba, who said in 1 Kings 9:1–9, "The half was not told me" of all the wisdom and answers to questions that Solomon gave her. In heaven we will greet the other half of what He's done. As I stand to give a graduation address, I know I am impacting another generation and the next after that.

And I know I will do this until I can function no more.

CHAPTER 24
Transitions and More Assignments

As I've surrendered to the Lord and allowed Him to land precious cargo on the runways of my heart through these many years, I'm honored and grateful for the kingdom work He's allowed me to participate in and the many people I've come to know and love through it.

Planning for the Future of Joshua Nations

In order for the ministry of Joshua Nations to continue, I realized I needed to put a plan of transition and succession into operation—a plan that would secure a lasting impact in the nations. I knew that it probably would be one of the most important decisions of my half of century of ministry, if not the most important. And if done well, I would join the cloud of witnesses to look down on those coming behind me to fulfill the Great Commission through Joshua Nations.

As I began the process, a large and wonderful missions organization expressed an interest in providing succession for Joshua Nations. They graciously extended that offer to us by meeting with us for a day to discuss that probability. They invited us to come under their ministry, but it seemed as though we were not ready to do so.

A couple of years later, I received a phone call from Jason Holland. He was interested in becoming my successor if I were interested. We spent a considerable amount of time together, discussing all the matters concerned in such a move. He and his wife, Anna, met with our board to consider this.

The board and I sensed this was the proper and right direction for Joshua Nations.

This was the beginning of a five-year process, and at launch of this book in October 2018, we are in the fourth year. We determined the time to pass the baton on is October 1, 2019.

In the transition, Jason came aboard, rolled up his sleeves to work, and has served wholeheartedly as Director of Operations for Joshua Nations. He and Anna are diligently serving the ministry. In 2018, they pulled up roots in Texas and moved to Arvada, Colorado, to more fully follow the call.

Jason is not a stranger to missions and comes highly qualified and with a heart for the Lord and serving people in the nations. He's a son of a Bible school dean, was raised in and surrounded by missions and ministry. His parents were given to the kingdom work. Then God whetted his heart for hands-on international missions when he served 13 years as international director of a large missions organization, Global Advance. His love for the nations grew as he traveled and trained leaders worldwide. As we traveled together, I witnessed his love and desire for people to come to know Jesus and grow in relationship to Him. As we ministered in many nations, I noticed his unmistakable penchant for the frontline hidden heroes.

I am so grateful God has given us Jason to continue the direction and leadership of Joshua Nations into the years to come. His ability to get things done, his forward thinking, his strategic mindset, creativity, and technological talents are an excellent fit for Joshua Nations. His leadership and prophetic bent cause him to be a great leader, and with great joy, I will pass the baton on to a very worthy servant of God.

And I'm not planning on disappearing from Joshua Nations even after Jason is fully in charge. As founder and former president, I will still be involved in the ministry in the years to come, and I look forward to continuing to travel, to train, and to equip leaders.

Seven New Assignments

Although 74 years old at the time of this writing, I encountered even more from the Holy Spirit following a 5-week trip in Africa recently. I returned home to 14 hours of sweet sleep. Just before I woke up I had a dream/vision.

The Holy Spirit spoke to me very clearly, *Multiply yourself in seven ways in these days.*

Of course I did the spiritual thing: I went back to sleep!

Sometime later, I woke up again, stumbled into the kitchen, got my Keurig cup of coffee and sat in my praying-meditating-reading chair.

The next three hours the Holy Spirit downloaded seven new and distinct assignments for my life. It was a life-altering experience, probably one of the greatest in the last 50 years. I then went to the Psalms to read again, "Teach [me] to number [my] days, that [I] may apply my heart unto wisdom" and began to map out the next 15 to 20 years.

I have already begun these assignments. Here they are:

> ### Fulfill Your Assignment
>
> God wants for all of us to multiply our gifts, our callings, and our work for him in this hour. Would you ask the Lord to speak to you about your remaining years of life? David said, "Teach me and make known to me the end and the measure of my days to apply my heart unto wisdom" (see Psalm 90:12 and Psalm 39:4). This is a valuable and vital prayer!
>
> Seek the Father for your assignment here on this earth. Then **pray, plot, and pursue!**
>
> —Pastor Russ Frase, March 2016 Newsletter

1. To video archive my speaking and teaching ministry
2. To establish Bible schools in the Denver Metro Area
3. To study and research and write books
4. To claim all of my family to God's purpose
5. To mentor seven distinct disciples
6. To develop a missions' mentoring program
7. To successfully complete the transition

So I've opened these seven new runways in my heart. I could be tempted to slow down, ease off, and just relax and live on easy street. But I know in my heart, God is giving me *more* assignments. For each of us, there will always be *more* until we close our eyelids for the last time. As Erwin McManus says, "Save nothing for the next world." Be sure that you have no more arrows in your quiver when that day comes. Then once we cross the divine divide, *more* will be awaiting us. And all through eternity there will be *more*.

The Lord told me: *Give your best in the capacity you have in the next 10 years.* And that's what I aim to do.

Our Future Is So Bright

Even as I continue to direct Joshua Nations, I've been moving forward in these seven assignments. The most recent of these new runways was the opportunity to tape 15 programs that will be televised and could reach 100 million viewers in 70 nations.

Years ago, when I visited Pakistan and we started a Bible school there, I met Pastor Nathaniel Barkat, who had established an orphanage, school, and feeding programs and had planted many churches there. One of his sons, Salik, studied in America with Marilyn Hickey's Bible school in Denver. Salik has now established an incredible ministry in Lahore, Pakistan, and is currently building a 3,000-seat church in that city. Even more fruitful is his Barkat Television, which reaches those 70 nations.

In May 2018, Jason Holland, Pastor George Morrison, Ken Yanke, and I traveled to give leadership seminars in Pakistan, preach at two churches, and participate in an open-air crusade to 11,000 spiritually hungry Pakistanis.

Amazingly, Pastor Salik also invited Joshua Nations to produce 15 programs on the Holy Spirit, which his ministry will televise. As of this writing, just yesterday we taped the last of those fifteen 27-minute programs! They will be dubbed into Urdu and viewed on that network.

The Holy Spirit is opening amazing doors for the Word of God to spread!

Also, we are preparing and taping the Joshua Nations curriculum for an online accredited Bible school. We are also establishing Joshua Nations schools in the Denver metroplex.

We also plan to train new Joshua Nations reps, which will allow us to develop more leaders around the world. In addition, we will more intentionally go to the unreached peoples in the nations who do not know Jesus.

We will continue to collaborate with Diane Brask of Seed Planters International in her Storytelling Revolution in the future. She has conducted storytelling seminars in 25 nations so far, as well as in America, and will continue to reach out to more ends-of-the-earth people. With her incredible gifts as a communicator, she has touched multitudes of lives with thousands coming to Christ and being discipled every year.

Amazing Results in Bolivia, August 2018

A couple of weeks ago, I returned with my team from Bolivia with great news:

- More than 3,000 made decisions for Jesus in the night crusades.
- We ministered to 2,300 leaders in morning and afternoon sessions— awesome!
- Carl Rogers helped me train 350 leaders to start BTCs.
- We gave out 2,400 sets of Joshua Nations curriculum.
- I released 17-year-old Joshua Hall to speak in one of the evening crusades, and he was outstanding! (We will train him as a Joshua Nations rep, part of the next generation, training leaders God is raising up to help leaders set up Bible Training Centers around the world!)

The Holy Spirit caused many amazing miracles in Bolivia—blind eyes were opened, tumors disappeared, and deaf ears could hear!

At this time in my life, the Lord continues to land *more* treasures on the runways of my heart—*more* revelation, scripture truths, and ministry experiences. The work of the Holy Spirit continues on and on. There is more for now and in the ages to come. We will never outgrow the desire and experience for *more* because the kingdom of God is without end.

CHAPTER 25

What Now?

Everything God has to offer is waiting to land on the runways of your heart. The Holy Spirit is waiting to execute the ways, will, and works of God and Jesus in your life and propel you to great heights into the fullness of His divine destiny for you.

The runways are different for everybody. And how the Holy Spirit speaks to each of us and works through us is individual and personalized. After studying more than 40 great worldwide Christian leaders from various denominations, I found they all agree that believers need the power of the Holy Spirit. They vary in their approaches and definitions of the infilling or baptism in the Holy Spirit, but all come to the starting gate with the same truth: One must be filled with or baptized in the Holy Spirit to have His power. This comes as we surrender to the Holy Spirit and let Him continually fill us (Ephesians 5:18).

Your openness to all the gifts and fruits of the Holy Spirit will allow the spiritual realities to crowd out everything else and position you to receive the best of the Father.

The Challenge

My hope is that—as you've followed my journey through the ups and downs, uncertain times, and joyous ones—this book is more than a 50-year collection of good stories for you. I sincerely hope it awakens your heart daily to the will of the Father and Jesus in your life. I pray you will not put *Runways of the Heart* on a shelf as a feel-good read, but that you realize that the Holy Spirit moves us from being benchwarmers to an active Spirit-filled role in the kingdom of God. We all are accountable as to how we steward the person, work, and ministry of the Holy Spirit. One cannot merely tip his hat to the Holy Spirit. Surrendering to Him and following Him is not an option in the life of a believer—we must be intentional.

Powerful Encounter on My Deck

When I travel for missions, I miss the in-depth devotional time in the intimacy with the Father, Son, and Holy Spirit I get when I spend several hours on my back deck with my Bible open in front of me. This is where everything is ignited in my spirit and soul. God is so blessed during these times, and He blesses me.

During one powerful encounter on my deck early one morning, I was praying for 30 minutes in my private prayer language and enjoying the beautiful presence of the Holy Spirit in worship. The sun was coming up, the birds were chirping, and I felt a slight breeze.

And all of a sudden I saw *them*. I had never seen them before. Two beautiful doves had settled in the tree branch next to my deck, and they were looking right me. I was taken aback and sensed that there was something the Holy Spirit wanted to say to me. I listened.

If you will build a nest for me, I will come and rest. A runway of rest that is a rest of created time with Me.

The Lord invited me to build a resting place in my heart for the Holy Spirit to occupy and abide.

This is my invitation to you, my friends. To daily build a place for the Holy Spirit. There you will find an intimacy found nowhere else. There you will receive from Him everything you need for every day. There you will receive wisdom, guidance, solutions, answers, and

Respond to God Quickly and Soar!

Anytime revelation comes, you've got to respond to it in some way. Either in your heart or by outward action.

The quicker you do that, then the quicker God can unfold all that He has for you. The next step. The next plan. The next vision. Your destiny. All it takes is one verse of scripture and God speaking through that to change the course of your life. To guide you to a new runway for takeoff.

New opportunities to soar higher in the Spirit are waiting for everybody. But we have to be open to it.

That's the crux of it all.

the equipping to serve everyone else. It is from these moments that you receive fresh infilling to release.

Jesus said that "from [our] innermost being will flow rivers of living water" (John 7:37–39, NASB). And He does not give us the Holy Spirit for us to keep but to release to others what He gives and does in us.

You get the best when you rest. That is, when you set aside times of intimacy with the Holy Spirit. But you have to do that—intentionally seek the Holy Spirit daily. As you build a place for Him to abide, your life will be mightily enhanced with all He has. It is His joy to bless you and for you to be a blessing. As we close this book, I invite you into a lifestyle of continuing to be filled by the Holy Spirit.

What if we stand before Jesus someday and He asks, "What did you do with My Holy Spirit?"

PART TWO
More Stories

Why We Include These Other Stories in the Book

By Marla Lindstrom Benroth
Collaborator on *Runways of the Heart*
Creative Journalist
Project Manager, Editor, and
Writer Trainer for Good Catch Publishing

As Pastor Russ and I collaborated on this book together (him sharing his amazing stories and passionate pursuit of the Holy Spirit while I digitally recorded them and took copious notes), I realized about two years into what turned out to be a four-and-a half-year project, something was missing. By talking just to Pastor Russ, I wasn't getting the depth of how people were affected by his zest for the Lord and the way he mined truths from the Holy Spirit and Word for their lives.

Okay, I grant you, maybe Pastor Russ did not know the far-reaching effects on many people of his selfless sacrifices. Maybe he just took for granted his welcoming attitude and roll-up-his-sleeves-come-alongside attitude and didn't realize it meant more to people than he thought. Most of us have no idea the impact our lives make on others, even in our little thoughtful gestures.

But at that stage in the project, I got tired of trying to read between the lines to get more depth from Pastor Russ—because he will not brag about himself! He is notorious for downplaying his role in matters.

And then the Lord through the Holy Spirit did an amazing thing. One day, I was sitting with Pastor Russ in his office listening to stories, recording them, taking notes, and asking questions.

"Lana and Nancy must have gotten back from lunch!" he exclaimed looking out the bay window.

Nancy? Did he mean Nancy, co-director of The Akha Outreach in Thailand? She's here?

The two of them walked in the door, and I said kinda quietly, "What I wouldn't give to talk to Nancy!"

"She's in town for a few days," he said.

I was very curious about her perspective on the relationship he had built with Nancy and Aje, her husband, through the many years. Pastor Russ spoke of Aje so fondly so many times, and I knew he visited them and their work in Thailand almost every year. It was because of Aje's request that he wrote the *Holy Spirit* manual. I was dying to talk to Nancy.

"Would you like to talk to her?" he asked.

"Yes, I would!"

Nancy sat across from me while Pastor Russ disappeared into another room. We talked for only 15 minutes that time, but that 15 minutes gave me insights that helped me to understand Pastor Russ in a way I hadn't even thought of. And, without him in the room, she freely shared from her heart.

"When the dean comes to our outreach in Thailand and stands before the students to teach, it's more than as a teacher," she told me in her quiet, steadfast voice. "He looks out at them with love, and his eyes tear up as he talks to them. They love him and see him as a grandfather in the faith. They miss his tears."

Nancy's words touched my heart deeply. *Tears like the Father. His passion for Jesus and for them perhaps touched these Thai students even more than the Word of God he brought.*

This was the Holy Spirit's way of opening up a whole new realm of possibilities for this book. My journalistic instincts kicked in, and I realized that it could help you readers to know Pastor Russ's story better through other peoples' eyes. People who have spent a lot of time with him, including serving alongside him and Lana in the States and overseas.

And I realized talking to them would help *me* get to know God's ways in and through his life better, too. (It did more than that. The runways on my heart expanded as I talked with these incredible, sold-out soldiers!)

Shortly after listening to Nancy, I asked Pastor Russ's permission to interview Joshua Nations reps, old friends, and anyone I could find that could help fill out his story. He gave me the green light. And he even gave me names and helped facilitate meetings with those who visited the Denver area from overseas, like John Wandera and Donato from Cuba.

You will find these stories sprinkled throughout the book as sidebars and in this Part Two section, gleaned from more than 50 hours of interviews with them. But I assure you, no one prompted them to say the positive things they said about how Pastor Russ encouraged them in some way. Those things just flowed from folks grateful for their relationship with this amazing man and for his inspiring surrender to the Holy Spirit.

And I captured them.

I hope these extra stories add to the richness of your understanding of how the Holy Spirit is at work in individual lives and around the world in beautiful and specific ways. And that they encourage you: it's not ability, but *availability* and *passion for more of Jesus* that are God's main requirements.

Say "Yes!" and partner with Him in His kingdom work—empowered by the Holy Spirit.

International Impact
The Dean as a Mentor and Father

Told by Nancy Kukaewkasem
Co-Director of the Akha Outreach Foundation in Thailand

My husband, Aje is much like Dean Frase (I call him that because we knew him as the dean of RMBI). They are very similar spirits. They both *love* learning. They love academics. They are brilliant men. But they sit with people right where they are and never make them feel stupid. They have a way of really honoring and valuing people.

The scriptures say, "He [God] will turn the hearts of the fathers to their children and the children's hearts to their fathers" (Malachi 4:6, NLT). The biggest injury in our country is the loss of fathers. Dean Frase mentored Aje, and he continues to be a father to him. He visits us in Thailand frequently and speaks into our lives and into the lives of the students, who consider him a "grandfather" at the Akha Outreach mission.

How Aje and I Met

I was born in the US. In my mid-20s, I ministered to girls at risk for prostitution in Chiang Rai in Northern Thailand and hosted YWAM teams who traveled to villages providing humanitarian services. It was on one of those trips that I met Aje. He'd come to know the Lord as a teen when an evangelist asked, "Do you want a friend that can be with you at all places and all times?" Studying in a crowded and sparse dorm, he wondered, *Who wouldn't want that?* He grew in his faith by traveling as a translator with a Thai pastor.

His father was chief of the largest Akha village in Thailand and was a man of great foresight who sent his young sons to school in the city when no one else in the village would dare. Aje received citizenship just two days before entering the university. And he earned a four-year degree.

The more I learned about him, the more I appreciated his heart and his passion for his people.

Unlike others, he wanted to take everything he learned back to his village to help his people. That drew me to him.

One day, Aje asked me, "How long are you going to be in Thailand?"

I told him, "Five years."

"How about making it 50?" That was his proposal!

I loved him and the people and readily agreed to marry him.

Needing More Bible Training

Aje told me one day, "As I meet people's physical needs, I see they have greater needs spiritually. But I can only take them as far as I've grown in the Lord. I need more Bible training …"

So, while I continued my work with the people in Thailand, he attended YWAM's Discipleship Training School (DTS) in Sydney, Australia.

Then I heard Dean Frase was starting Rocky Mountain Bible Institute in my home church.

"This would be a great way for you to get to know Faith Bible Chapel and receive mentoring," I told him.

Things happened fast. After he returned from DTS, we flew to Colorado the summer of 1994, married, and we both planned to start attending RMBI. After listening to one of Dean Frase's sermons (he was fired up and preaching fast!), Aje told me sadly in Ackhan, "I don't know if I can keep up with him. My English isn't that good. And I've never studied in English."

Newly married, both of us working part-time jobs, we both enrolled in RMBI. For me to get my homework done and then help my husband translate and learn was hard for both of us. And, though reasonable, the tuition was too expensive for us.

I decided to switch to the layman's weekly FBC School of the Bible, help Aje translate his studies, and work full time. Aje proudly walked across the stage and received his two-year diploma in that first graduating class of 1994.

Aje grew spiritually under the dean's authority at RMBI. About three to six months after he'd graduated, we attended a casual picnic at the dean's house. A student said to me, "I miss the tears of the dean." Dean Frase's love for the Bible and for people greatly impacted my husband. He wasn't teaching just to be teaching. He was teaching to impart. To release something. He did it with great passion.

Dean Frase Is an Encouraging Mentor

After Aje and I raised support, we started our ministry together in Thailand. The dean flew to our mission on a yearly basis. He spoke into our lives—he always seemed to have a word that came from God two to three years out for us, like when he saw how Aje had begun a program with pastors in the area.

"You know you are going to have to start your own church," he told us on one of his early visits. "You are raising up leaders, but there's no platform or place for them to be empowered and grow. You are eventually going to have to start a church in order to give a healthy environment to the leaders you are raising up."

Sure enough, we started a church three years after he predicted we would.

More Insights

Dean Frase is one of the most gracious people I know. But he notices things. Even today, when we need to make a big decision, it's the dean we Skype to talk. He never says, "You have to do this," or, "You should do that." He asks hard questions—he almost pulls the answer from within you.

The biggest challenge for anyone in ministry is managing people, managing your staff. He first starts with "How are things at home? How are things in the relationship between the two of you? Are you getting enough breaks and family time? How are things with your staff?"

He's the first one who said to us, "You get what you tolerate. If you don't address issues and speak the truth in love, you'll pay for it."

He tells us this in a very private, gentle conversation.

I don't think I've ever heard him complain. Certain guests might say, "The beds are too hard. If only I could have this …"

When he arrives at our Akha Outreach, he is not demanding at all. He's quick to humbly offer his services. "Wherever you want me to go, whatever you want me to do." Just recently—he's in his 70s—he requested after he flew 26 hours from the United States to Thailand, "Just give me a day's rest."

His heart is to encourage, even if it is just coming and listening to other preachers and encouraging them.

Like "Father" Like "Son"

There are times when I see the dean put his faith in someone and I think, *That looks pretty shaky to me! I don't know if I would have chosen that individual for that job.*

But it's as though the person thinks, *The dean believes in me?* and then lives up to his or her potential.

The dean pulled that ability out of Aje, to believe in people before they've proven themselves. There's such a kindred spirit between the two.

One of my greatest joys is to watch the dean preach a message and Aje translate it. They both get so excited about it, and they flow with each other in a beautiful anointing of the Spirit together. And they have such a good time feeding off one another.

Our relationship with the dean continues to impact our lives in huge ways, and I always look forward to spending time with Lana and Dean Frase.

Impact in the US
RMBI Gave Me Focus
for God's Call On My Life

Told by Scott Applegate
Pastor, Novation Church in Westminster, Colorado

I chased rock 'n' roll and baseball before God caught me, saved me, and put in my heart a desire to pastor a church. But a lot happened in my life between the call and the commission as pastor.

God used RMBI in a huge way in my life to prepare me and lead me on His path: Pastor Russ as a mentor, the books we read, friendships I forged with fellow classmates, and the teachers there who challenged and influenced my thinking. And then the opportunity later to teach classes there.

I started attending RMBI at age 25 soon after it started and almost quit after the first year. I prayed a lot: should I quit and serve the Lord as a businessman? Am I supposed to go into full-time ministry and preach? I sensed Him encouraging me to finish school.

Pastor Russ and the students gave me a lot of encouraging, prophetic words, but those didn't start sinking in until the second year. Dr. Dannie Fisher (who took over the pastorate of Faith Bible Chapel Southwest and whom Pastor Russ brought to teach at RMBI, too) confirmed for me one day what I felt in my heart: "The word of the Lord is that you'll know as you follow along." Follow Him. One step at a time, even though I didn't know where he'd lead. Seems like He speaks to me a lot like that.

Halfway through RMBI, Tim Lovell, FBC's youth pastor, asked me to bring my guitar and play at meetings. I resisted working with the high school youth, but did help out, as I did with many other ministries. After graduating, my heart for the youth warmed, and I dropped the other ministries to work with Tim and the kids. When he broke his neck skiing right before a mission trip to San Salvador he'd planned to take the youth on, I was thrown into leading the students that week—and learned a lot!

After RMBI Graduation

I graduated from RMBI in 1994 in the first graduating class. When Pastor George asked Tim to lead young adults, he put me in charge of the youth group. I also preached on Wednesday nights and served and learned about a broad range of church ministries. I went on staff at FBC in 1996.

I desired to one day teach at RMBI, and Pastor Russ encouraged me to continue on with my education to prepare me for that. RMBI credits transferred to Trinity College of the Bible and Seminary, and from there I got my master's from another institute.

Pastor Russ then gave me classes to teach and helped me in huge ways, mentoring me through the curriculum and how to interact with and minister to the students. I taught Spiritual Development, New Testament Survey, and the Pastoral Epistles.

Around 2011, as my wife Janell prayed, she felt the Lord leading me to start a church, and I confirmed that in my heart. With Pastor George's blessing in 2012, we started Novation Church in the Denver area. I'd learned so much and now saw God's timing to fulfill the deepest desire of my heart: pastor a church.

Pastor Russ came alongside and helped me in those early days.

We chose to support him and Joshua Nations as our first overseas ministry. It's ironic and great that we get to support his ministry after all he did for me.

I've observed the other students who attended with me and have kept up with some even today—RMBI was like a proving ground. I'd tell people who felt a nudge toward ministry in general to go through RMBI and they'd find confirmation there one way or another.

Attending RMBI changed the course of my life. Pastor Russ had deep convictions of how he did things, but never expected RMBI students to be carbon copies of him. He encouraged—and today encourages—people to fulfill their own individual destinies, being who we are with the giftings God's given us.

Behind-the-Scenes Warriors

Told by Lanette Glover
Member of Joshua Nations' Asia Rep,
Bobbie Stratman's Team of Intercessors

God put Bobbie and me together in a special way around 2007. One month before she headed to Asia after Pastor Russ invited her to represent Joshua Nations, Bobbie—in her passionate way—told me she would be training leaders how to start Bible Training Centers. Something in my heart leapt as I listened, totally enthralled. She'd recruited several people to pray for her, and I'd be number five on the team with more to come several years later.

This started me on a journey I could have never foreseen. For Bobbie, her intercessors are like gold. She treats us like important partners and tells us she cannot do what she does without us. She is in constant communication with us via email or Skype when out of the country and in person when she comes home.

Her intercessor team, now expanded, with Lorel Zander leading it, meets every month to pray corporately, and we carry around a list of requests to pray in our private times. One year, she asked me to teach about the power of communion (the Lord's Supper) and for a period of time one summer, each of us took communion in our quiet times before the Lord every day and prayed not only for the ministry, but also for people we knew. The Lord physically healed quite a number of people during that time!

Bobbie engages us intimately in the Joshua Nations' mission God's called her to, and we know it is a calling for us, too.

She's taught us a lot about the power of prayer. When she comes into town, we'll gather for extended times: praying and fasting together at Praise Mountain or at Dee Nance's cabin in Grand Lake for a weekend. Or we'll gather for an all-night meeting at my home. We'll trace Bobbie's journey on the map and take pages of notes and prayer requests—times of blessing and spiritual growth for all of us.

I have to think we knock on heaven's gates and make a difference in the lives of people across the ocean.

I found that when Bobbie returned to the US, she needed to share everything on her heart and receive emotional support from us, too, before heading back. She needs us for more than just behind-the-scenes prayer support. A lady so gifted of the Lord, Bobbie will speak into each of our lives, minister to us, and prophesy over us.

Bobbie is more than our special missionary—she models true friendship. And it's not a surface relationship. We not only encourage one another, but we challenge each other, too, asking the tough questions. That's a necessary part when discovering God's will in a matter and for our lives.

One would think that agreeing to pray for someone serving the Lord like Bobbie would be a huge sacrifice, and it is to an extent. But it has blessed *me* and helped *me* grow beyond what I could have ever imagined. I'm a quiet person, but as Bobbie saw my gift of teaching, she invited *me* to come to China and teach! I joined her and a small team on two mission trips. In America, there are so many qualified teachers, you may not get to use your giftings. But overseas, they are so hungry. "The harvest is ripe but the laborers are few" (Matthew 9:37).

On one of those trips, I had the awesome opportunity to travel with Bobbie, Pastor Russ, and also his wife, Lana. My daughter, Hannah, came with us on the second trip, and that was a huge blessing. One of my favorite photos of all time is of Hannah and me sitting with a live panda bear between us. He's only a year old and munching on a bamboo stick. Oh! The opportunities that come with saying yes! God gives back in abundant ways.

Those two trips completely changed my perspective on missions. When I compare the poverty with America's wealth, I have to ask myself, "Why was I chosen to be so blessed in the place where I live?"

Because Bobbie invited and encouraged *me* to use my God-given gift of teaching, I've become more aware of it and want to find opportunities to teach more in the US.

I encourage people to invest themselves personally in a missionary. Not just giving financially. Engage. Write notes, hold prayer meetings. Ask how you can bring your gifts to the table to help—whether you are a businessperson, talented in the creative arts, medicine, or any other way.

This journey with Bobbie and Joshua Nations has been an awesome one for me, beyond what I could have imagined! I liken it to a story in Exodus 17:10–13 (NLT):

> So Joshua did what Moses had commanded and fought the army of Amalek. Meanwhile, Moses, Aaron, and Hur climbed to the top of a nearby hill. As long as Moses held up the staff in his hand, the Israelites had the advantage, but whenever he dropped his hand, the Amalekites gained the advantage. Moses' arms soon became so tired he could no longer hold them up. So Aaron and Hur found a stone for him to sit on. Then they stood on each side of Moses, holding up his hands. So his hands held steady until sunset. As a result, Joshua overwhelmed the army of Amalek in battle.

We are overcoming the enemy together!

A Well-Used Word

Told by Greg Johnsen
Joshua Nations Rep and Intercessor since 2011
Contractor in the Construction Industry

By 2018, I'd gone with Pastor Russ on more than 13 mission trips. The first one was to Pakistan just after 9-11, and it was just Russ and I because of all the complications of overseas travel for others who'd planned on going.

We've been in some very dangerous places and eaten awful food and slept on uncomfortable mats in places where big bugs don't sleep. We've ministered to a double-decker busload of people whose bus suddenly turned over on a primitive dirt road in Sierra Leone, Africa. I've also had the humble honor of being the recipient of grateful people in Cuba who took up an offering and gave us what little they had so those in other nations could hear the gospel.

Pastor Russ's love for reading the Bible has impacted me, and it is because of his immersion in the Word of God that I feel safe. I've noticed that wherever we travel, when he is not in a conversation with someone or preparing in some way, he is reading his Bible.

One morning, as we flew to Ghana, Africa, I woke up on the plane at 3:00 a.m. The cabin was quiet and dark. I looked across the aisle and saw a little light shining in the corner. There was Russ, his glasses down on the end of his nose, his tablet with the Bible on it lit up as he read. That's when I knew I was safe on any trip with him as our authority and guide.

I said to him one time, "It seems like you don't have any down time. You are always reading the Word."

He replied, "Greg, in the position God's called me to, I can't ever afford to let my mind be blank. I can't just let it wander. If I'm not doing something constructive for the kingdom, I need to read the Word. Battles are won and lost in the mind. I can't just sit and let my mind be idle. That way, the enemy can't get me and destroy the call on my life."

I never forgot that. He's imparted that love for the Word of God to me and many others.

"For the Word of God is living and powerful, and sharper than any two-edged sword, piercing even to the division of soul and spirit, and of joints and marrow, and is a discerner of the thoughts and intents of the heart" (Hebrews 4:12).

Russ's Prophetic Words
Propelled Me into Destiny

Told By Jack Gaudin
Joshua Nations Rep to 30 Nations
Former Businessman in Oil & Gas
Founder, Freedom Through Faith Ministries, www.ftfm.org

I connected with Russ through the pastor of my Denver church, Praise Church, in the 1990s. After 21 years in the oil and gas industry, I took a leap of faith and retired at age 41. I sensed a call from God to prepare for missions, though I wasn't sure what, and enrolled in RMBI. I attended from 1995 to 1997, quite a different experience from career to studying with 18- to 20-year-olds.

I'd seen Russ move prophetically at my church, giving accurate words of encouragement and exhortation and speaking true words to people I knew. I'd begun to doubt my decision to leave my lucrative job, wondering if I'd really heard from the Lord. So I perked up one morning my first semester at RMBI when he said during our morning devotions, "I've got a treadmill word for you, Jack!"

A "treadmill word"? What is that?

"The Lord gave it to me while on my treadmill this morning," he explained. "You've made many decisions before this, but now, in surrendering to the Lord's will, there will be provision."

That encouraged me to keep moving forward, completing certification at RMBI. While attending school, I served in Faith Bible Chapel's jail ministry at Denver City Jail a few times, then with a team from Praise Church at the Jefferson County jail. A desire to share the good news of Christ and salvation he offered to prisoners burned in my heart. I moved on to the Denver

Reception and Diagnostic Center, the first stop for all offenders sentenced to the Department of Corrections.

After I graduated, I was offered a job as chaplain at the Colorado State Penitentiary in the Super Max (where the most hardened criminals are incarcerated). It was largely volunteer, so I raised support, and my wife Debbie and 5-year-old son moved to Cañon City.

It was overwhelming, physically and mentally—and lonely. I didn't belong to either camp, the staff or the restless inmates. The staff didn't know me or automatically trust me, and the inmates, under lockdown 23 hours a day, tested me. We'd left a nice home in southwest Denver for a small rental in the hot desert. I began to doubt if I'd made the right decision in moving the family two hours south.

Questions bombarded me: *Should I beg my former boss for my job back? Are these men—the worst of the worst of Colorado—worth me moving my family here?* While sipping a cup of coffee one morning, the Lord spoke. *Jack, that's who I gave My life for!* I winced.

In the sanctuary at Praise Church one Sunday while visiting, I stepped in at the end of a long line of people waiting for Russ to pray and prophesy over them. Not too eager, my reserved denominational background held me at bay.

Russ walked down the line, praying with passion and heart for each person. He knew nothing of how I'd been feeling as prison chaplain in Cañon City. He stopped in front of me and said:

> *This is the time.*
> *This is the place.*
> *This is the season, My son.*
> *Never doubt it!*

This prophetic word changed my life. Instantly, all doubt left me. I stopped being double-minded, wondering if I'd missed God and if I should try to get my old job back.

From that moment on, I rolled up my sleeves. "This is where I'm supposed to be!" I declared walking through the resounding corridors of the prison. "Let's get to work!"

Because of that timely encouraging word from Russ that pierced my heart with truth from the Holy Spirit, the enemy could not use these doubts against me.

I served as chaplain for 10 years, given the incredible privilege of seeing many saved, delivered, healed, and filled with the Spirit. And later, discipled.

The Lord called me out of the prison to international missions and an invitation around 2007 from Russ—a whirlwind trip through five nations in two-and-a-half weeks, extended to six weeks—sealed the deal and launched me into a new level of ministry.

I've now been on 45 trips to 30 nations training pastors and leaders how to start Joshua Nations Bible Training Centers, and teaching on and ministering healing. It's hard to believe! About half of them, as I recall, have been with Pastor Russ.

90 Minutes from Arrest

Told by an Anonymous Joshua Nations Rep

After a wonderful breakfast at our quaint downtown hotel in a region of Asia, we waited for our host to arrive, now more than an hour late. Multiple attempts to locate him through text messages proved unsuccessful.

Finally, with a look of grave concern, he stood before us.

"We must *pray!*" he said.

"Sure. Why?"

Our dear brother and host said, "The police came early and arrested all the tribal leaders!" He explained that police don't typically come so early in the morning, but often wait until at least 10:00 a.m. for maximum impact. Had the police raided the event at that time or later, *all* of us, would have been arrested. We would have been deported and never allowed to return. I am so grateful how God's hand protected us.

Knowing the gravity of the situation, we prayed right then and there. Not bowing our heads. Not holding hands in a circle. But, like we do in so many volatile locations, we prayed with our heads up and eyes open so as to appear like we were in regular conversation. And, despite the situation, God gave us great peace and calm through this storm.

Our host left for the police station to see what could be done to free those who had been arrested. Off and on for the next 40 hours while we prayed, he negotiated with the police. By God's grace, and a payment of "bail," authorities released the men and women. Unfortunately, many of our leaders were forced to return to their villages and forgo the training they had so eagerly awaited. The training moved to another location, and only 30 of the more than 80 leaders remained.

Although the event was smaller and shorter than we anticipated, it was a success! We equipped those leaders to begin Joshua Nations Bible Training Centers in their villages and areas of influence in that region.

Training Leaders in Mexico

Told by Carl & Lani Rogers
Joshua Nations Reps to Mexico
Founders of Christ for Life International
Directors of Faith Bible Chapel's Healing Room

We've known Pastor Russ since around 1998. When we heard about Joshua Nations and what Pastor Russ was doing through it, it really intrigued us.

We'd been going to Mexico for many years and fell in love with the Mexican culture and people. We eventually bought our own condo so we had a base camp for ministry work and a place to vacation. We traveled to Mexico so often that we said, "Hey, we're here! Why not do something substantial for the Lord?"

We approached Pastor Russ about starting Bible Training Centers there.

Puerto Vallarta, Mexico

Our first step was to ask Pastor Russ to travel with us to Puerto Vallarta to introduce Joshua Nations and teach the pastors and leaders how to start BTCs. The pastor of the church we attended there connected us with Pastor Luis Miguel. We set the training up at his church (a building with a canvas tent outside for the church service). It was hot—like, you-are-sweating-constantly hot—and Pastor Russ trained about 12 pastors in the area. At the same time, we learned the process so we could train more leaders in the future.

The encouragement, inspiration, and tools Pastor Russ provided in that training planted seeds that are still bringing fruit. The leaders appreciate the simple, structured JN curriculum that anyone can use. And Pastor Luis has run with it.

Pastor Luis has grown so much personally in the time we've known him. And his church has grown. He's received great favor with the city. With city approval, he's completing work on a community center. The lower level is the church sanctuary; the second and third levels are used for JN training, computer classes, English classes, and community activities. They also provide weekly feeding programs for children.

We see our role, besides the leadership training and teaching healing, as encouragers, not only to the pastors and leaders, but to people in the churches. We minister to about six local Mexican churches whenever possible. God has also given us the opportunity to bring principles of unity to churches where there's been discord.

We attribute the results to that seed that Pastor Russ planted, because that seed got us *involved*, and the fruit of a seed spreads wide.

Pastors in Mexico City

In 2017, we took Pastor Russ and Pastor George Morrison to Mexico City. We rented a conference center and presented Joshua Nations to more than 200 pastors and church leaders. We pray that with the many seeds planted there we will see a new harvest of Bible schools throughout Mexico.

We love working with Joshua Nations. Pastor Russ is so gifted to train leaders and send them out. That's what he's done with us. He believes in us, encourages us, and has empowered us to train and work with pastors and leaders in Mexico. And that frees us to be available and let the Holy Spirit lead us to where we sense God wants us to serve.

From Witch Doctor's Son
to Son of the Most High God

Told by John Wandera
Native Regional Leader of BTCs in
Uganda, Kenya and the Congo

My mom was a witch doctor.

In 1981, at age 16 when a visiting preacher came to our school, I was converted along with 62 other students.

When I went back home to share this with my parents, they said I'd joined a false religion. I faced a very, very tough life. I worked in people's fields to raise money to pay my own school fees in secondary school (which included through high school) and to buy clothes.

I walked 26 kilometers one way to church every Sunday. No shoes. No bicycle. But I had a great passion to know and obey Christ. The experience was so real to me: I'd become a new creation, no longer the John I used to be. The John who didn't care, the John who did everything he wanted to do and went anywhere he wanted to go. The *new* John wanted to please Christ, my Lord, and do the will of the Father.

And I wanted others to experience this, too. God began raising me up to evangelize at school. The number of followers of Jesus grew from 63 students to 150. This is how my ministry began—the headmaster's children even became Christians! We were converting the whole school to Christ.

Where I came from, after practice teaching for a while without any further education, you are allowed to teach. So I taught for three years. Then I went into full-time ministry because of my passion to serve God and reach the unreached people and disciple them in the truth. Pastors and the man who led me to Christ mentored me. I moved to Nairobi, Kenya, for leadership training in a theological college for four years. Then I received further training in New Zealand for two years.

I'm married to one wife and she is a woman! Jesca and I married December 5, 1987, and we now have 22 children. Yes, 22! Four biological and 18 adopted.

How the JN Curriculum Changes Lives in Africa

Around 2013, I met Jack Gaudin, who introduced me to Russ Frase. He gave me a copy of the curriculum, and I studied it. I thought it was very, very simple and understandable. It was properly laid out. It didn't have tough, confusing theological words. I noticed how it cut across every denomination—all in the Body of Christ could benefit from it.

I knew I wanted to join with Joshua Nations and help set up Bible Training Centers in my country.

Uganda is 60 percent illiterate. So far, we've translated the materials into five local dialects to make it easier to reach my people and for them to get rooted in the Word of God.

How has learning and following this curriculum changed my life and the lives of others? Well, take my family for instance. Africa is different than the West. Culturally, an African man cannot walk hand-in-hand with his wife. He walks *farrrrrr ahead* with the wife behind, following.

And sitting at the same table with the family to eat food—no, no! The husband sits at the table by himself, and the wife sits on the floor with the children. So the husband is like the *king* of the home! I learned how to do that from my father.

But people we know testify, "John's family is different." I walk hand-in-hand with my wife. Though the table is too small for our 22 children, we crowd in as many as we can fit.

Many African men beat their wives. Because they claim they bought them with a dowry—so many cows—they treat a wife as property. But that is not me. I value my wife. I've never abused her. I treat her like a queen, actually. She is very happy. Very, very happy. Because of how I've learned how Christ treats people. That is why she is able to stand in and take care of the family while I am in the United States for this trip.

Jesca has studied the Joshua Nations curriculum—the first and second year. She uses that very model to teach the other women as she interacts with them in the village.

And my children have a different mindset than others at school. Once on her way from school, one of my daughters heard a couple arguing and came to us, exclaiming, "Why are they doing that? We never see it in our house. Go and help them!"

I take some of my children when they are on school break to Bible Training Centers with me to show them how I do this.

Starting BTCs in More Countries

So far, I am overseeing 35 training centers in Uganda, Kenya, and the Congo, as well as graduating students from a huge refugee camp in northwest Uganda that serves refugees from five countries.

We are setting up BTCs on the islands of one of the largest freshwater lakes in the world, Lake Victoria (bordered by Kenya, Rwanda, Burundi, DRC, Tanzania, and Uganda), where millions of people live. It is my hope and prayer that people from the BTCs we set up will send leaders to train and set up BTCs on more islands.

The Holy Spirit's Gift Boxes:
Tongues and Interpretation

A pastor, using Dr. Russ Frase's *Holy Spirit* manual, taught his congregation at a midweek service. The topic: the gifts of tongues and interpretation. He'd arranged boxes on the stage with the names of the gifts of the Spirit on each:

The Gifts of Power
Faith
Working of Miracles
Gift(s) of Healing

The Gifts of Revelation
Word of Wisdom
Word of Knowledge
Discerning of Spirits

The Gifts of Inspiration
Prophecy
Tongues
Interpretation of Tongues

At the end of his message, he invited those who wanted a particular gift to come and take that box. People walked to the stage and took boxes.

"There is a lady here who believes she has a message in tongues to give over the microphone," the pastor's wife said to him.

Hesitantly, not knowing how this would go down, the pastor handed the mike over to a lady wearing purple, and from her mouth poured a beautiful language, not English.

There'd better be an interpretation! the pastor thought, his eyes scanning the congregation hopefully. Fifteen seconds seemed like 15 minutes to him as his heart nearly beat out of his chest.

Another lady, with a rose-embossed white scarf, stood, took the mike, and began speaking in English—a beautiful interpretation that resonated with the pastor and his people, catalyzing a sense of freedom and spiritual power.

Neither lady had ever publicly spoken in tongues or interpreted tongues before.

Earlier, the lady in purple had chosen the box marked "Tongues." The lady with the rose scarf had chosen the box marked "Interpretation."

Mentoring Men on the
Power of the Holy Spirit in India

By Jason Holland
Executive Vice President for Joshua Nations
Future Director of Joshua Nations

India holds a special place in my heart. I've served and led teams to serve this nation and its people for 20 years—more than any other place on earth.

Around 2008, I led a team to North India to a city named Chandigarh. I'd visited and ministered in this city numerous times prior to this trip. At the request of a colleague in ministry, I took two men with me who had never been to India. These two brothers in the Lord had never experienced such idolatry and spiritual oppression, and until this trip had never experienced the Holy Spirit's power like they did. As a person who has seen the Holy Spirit move supernaturally on a frequent basis, I knew these men's lives would change on this trip.

In preparation, I did my best to coach them and set some expectations. I informed these dear brothers that it was highly likely that they would see and experience things like never before. From previous times, I knew that God would show up in power and lives would be transformed!

On our first day, we visited an orphanage stationed at a pastor's home in a rural village outside of Chandigarh. The pastor, his wife, and the 15 or so children living there under his care greeted us warmly, smiling and laughing. But I noticed one little boy about eight or nine years old who seemed like he was dealing with something more than just being sad or in a depressed mood. Often the Holy Spirit will give me discernment when people are dealing with different spiritual attacks, bondage, oppression, or even possession. Before the two brothers next to me responded to pray, I sensed the Holy Spirit leading me to raise an authoritative voice from 15 feet across the room.

"I command you, spirit of stupor, to be gone in Jesus name! Life, come back to this boy right now!" The boy blinked a couple times, and his countenance immediately changed as the oppressing spirit disappeared!

On our second day, at the request of the local pastors in Chandigarh, we drove to their newly purchased apartment home, happy to pray over it. Although this home was new to this pastor's family, a Hindu priest had owned it. After moving into the home, the pastor's family had not experienced a restful night of sleep. Every night they experienced various spiritual attacks, such as random strange noises, inanimate objects moving around their home, and even appearances of demonic spirits.

As we entered their apartment, we could feel that the atmosphere was not one of peace.

"What are we supposed to do?" my teammates asked me. "We have never been asked to pray over empty rooms and command the evil spirits to leave. This is not something that our denomination really talks about."

With a little instruction and guidance, they gladly obliged and began to walk through the home, one room at a time praying for God's presence to manifest and for God to cast out all demonic spirits and oppression. All of us together, including the pastor and his wife, walked through the home and prayed. We anointed the doors, windows, thresholds, and even the walls. After about 30 minutes of prayer, we sensed a tangible difference in the atmosphere.

The next morning, the pastor told us that, glory be to God, God had delivered their home from all demonic oppression, and for the first time, they slept soundly. The next night, they brought their children into the home, and again they slept without any issue.

God's authority, peace, and power reigned in this home after our time of prayer.

Astounded at this, the two brothers asked me many questions each night that we were together. Much to my delight, we discussed the Holy Spirit, spiritual gifts, and the power of God. They asked about the baptism of the Holy Spirit and speaking in tongues. It was my honor to encourage them in the pursuit of the baptism in the Holy Spirit.

Within a month or so of returning from India, each one of these brothers had a powerful encounter with Holy Spirit with the evidence of speaking in tongues. One of these men continued to pursue and dig deeper into the things of the Spirit. The next couple of months he matured more and more in his understanding and desire. By the end of a year, he was not only speaking in tongues, but also having prophetic dreams, visions, and words of knowledge.

It is a great joy for me to see God move supernaturally and to participate as His people discover the Holy Spirit's amazing power and presence.

Runways of the RMBI Graduates to the Nations

By Dr. Russ Frase, Jr.

O f the 500 students who graduated from Rocky Mountain Bible Institute, approximately 45 percent entered into full-time or part-time international and stateside missions or local church ministry. With my continuing relationships with many of the students in the US in the years since RMBI closed, I'd fuel my jet and fill it with resources—books, study materials, financial provision, spiritual and personal encouragement—to take to them on a regular basis while maintaining our relationships, a great joy to me!

Only eternity will register the impact of RMBI and what God has done through those whom He brought into our classrooms. It is my great honor and privilege to work alongside so many incredible servants of the Lord all around the world during the last 26 years. *Faithful* describes all of them. I think the greatest impact of RMBI was on me as a person and a leader. The students taught me so much, and those were most blessed and fruitful years. It is a joy to still be involved in many of their lives and ministries.

When the Bible institute opened, I told students a lifelong principle of mine: that I was committed to them all the way to Jesus coming or my going. I have ascribed to a truth I read many years ago. If you are not a king, be a kingmaker. I love filling the role of kingmaker. I love to open doors for others and help them get where the Lord wants them to be and do what they are supposed to do.

It has been a joy to mentor and guide them and sheer joy to see them prosper and extend their influence through so many more. Time, circumstances, and distance have separated many of us. Without fail, when I run across a former student, whether in ministry or not, they say, "Rocky Mountain Bible Institute was the best two years of my life."

I carry so many memories in my heart, so many stories and, I'm sure, quite a few from a memory that needs jogging. We added this at the end of the book, and I have, I am sure, missed somebody or your story. I will gladly add it to our second edition.

Ron and June Ammerman came to RMBI at retirement age. A tall stack of books waited for them on their desks when they walked into that first class in 1992. Ron carried two big book bags, one in each hand to balance his load as he walked out of class that first day. A few days after the first class, he came into my office with tears saying, "Dean Frase, I can't do this. I haven't been in school for 40 years."

I looked into his eyes and said, "It will be fine." He soon improved his grades from C's to A's as I expected.

Little did Ron and all of the others know how inadequate I felt as a teacher. This new position, running a Bible institute, greatly intimidated me. My only hope for success was to trust the Lord and take it one day at a time.

Ron and June went on to serve in many deprived nations for more than 20 years, forsaking the comforts of America for dire and difficult circumstances. June became a midwife and served with Ron faithfully with the ministry God had given her. Ron once told me about a particular Bangladesh event where the rats were crawling in the thatch roof at night, and in order to sleep and survive, he had to catch them and dispose of them (drown them in a bucket—ugh!). I treasure my ongoing relationship with Ron and June. We have traveled to Cuba many times and meet for breakfast from time to time.

I will never forget the day, a few days after graduation, when **Dustin Campbell** came into my office with great excitement. He exclaimed, "Dean Frase, I am going to the Philippines to be a missionary.

"How are you going to get there?" I asked.

"I have half of my airfare already."

I took out my checkbook and wrote him a check for the remainder. It wasn't much later he went, unbeknownst to me with all his belongings in a garbage bag and very little money and one pair of tennis shoes. He fought against great opposition, but he answered the call and for 20 years served YWAM Philippines and other nations.

Along the way, he married a sweet and lovely Filipina wife, Haydee, who has been an awesome helpmeet. He now serves at a YWAM base in Charlotte and ministers in many other nations. It was always good to have him speak at RMBI when he was in the States.

It has been so rewarding to see him grow, mature, and minister in an excellent manner. It is always good to see him when he is in town. Often he calls me for counsel and advice and usually gives me the same.

Alex Schlussler became a very successful pastor in the Seventh Day Adventist denomination, earning a master's degree and teaching about Israel in many of their congregations. He also has taught worship seminars. I remember a trip to Thailand where he taught on worship. The Akha people were quite reserved, but by the end of the week they worshipped in dance! He has for many years been a faithful rabbi and pastor of a very large church. I will always remember him singing the Aaronic blessing during chapel at RMBI. He and his wife, Ange, have served the Lord faithfully. Sometimes we hook up in Miami when we take our annual trip into Cuba.

Alex's mother-in-law, **Marilyn Scott,** another graduate of RMBI, did something for Lana and me that we will never forget. One day after class she came to me and said, "Dean Frase, you need a 501c3 nonprofit organization."

I replied, "We really don't need one."

She insisted several times. She had the ability to look into our future and see that God was going to use us in such a way that such an entity would be needed. And better yet she said, "I want to pay for it." How could we protest such a kind and insightful offer?

It was her foresight and guidance that set up Joshua Ministries which would become Joshua Nations. What a blessing. God puts special people in our lives to fulfill His purposes. Since 1998, this organization has so advanced the kingdom in many, many ways.

Penny Ikner's eyewitness account as a child of the miracle of the newspaper editor who got up and walked during an Easter Sunday service is told in Chapter 13. I led her to Christ in Athens, Texas, when she was seven. By "coincidence," her grandmother enrolled her in Rocky Mountain Bible

Institute from the East Coast, and we reunited. She had the privilege of meeting many RMBI students during the first four years and said that was a pivotal time that set the spiritual course of her life.

Penny continued her education and received her bachelor's degree in nursing and master's in nursing administration. She is the financial administrator of her church in Kennett Square, Pennsylvania. This is my Penny in pigtails! She has also joined teams with me on several mission trips and carries great love for the nations. Her continual friendship enriches Lana and me.

An ardent student of the Bible, **Scott Applegate**, after leaving RMBI, continued his education and earned his Bachelor's and Masters degrees. He served as associate pastor at Faith Bible Chapel for 15 years and then planted Novation church in 2013. This is a vibrant and active church with more than 400 in its community at this publication. It's a joy to listen to him teach and watch him shepherd his flock. Lana and I attend his church as often as we can, and I meet him for coffee to talk about our lives and ministries.

One Sunday morning, I was surprised that it seemed like an RMBI reunion when at least five graduates showed up at a service. We had fun reconnecting! Scott also has authored a great book titled, *Noblesse Oblige,* French for "noble obligation" that gives practical and inspiring direction for finding God's calling.

Scott Pearson planted Faith Bible Chapel Boulder County and teaches at BridgeWay Church in Denver. He has traveled with many international leaders in bringing deliverance and healing to many. The Lord uses Scott to talk to people anywhere, pray for them, and minister to them the miracle touch of Jesus. He is faithful to move in signs and wonders. We have been in the nations together.

Robert Quintana has pastored Pilgrim Congregational Church in inner city Denver for 10 years, has a feeding program to the community, and an annual youth outreach that draws many churches from across America working with him. Robert and I have worked closely together to see his church flourish. We talk and counsel via phone or during lunch. Hundreds have come to Christ. He has traveled with us to Cuba, and is a favorite preacher in the Cuban churches. We gather to "theologue" often over a meal. He is the theologian and I just listen. When I have a question about a biblical issue I call Robert.

While attending RMBI, **Jason Horning** was a youth pastor and ministered to hundreds of youth every week. He parked his truck by a local high school with a sign, "Let's talk," and offered a free coke and touched so many lives. He has planted a vibrant and powerful congregation in Leadville and has pastored the church for the last five years. I remember he came to me with questions about the baptism in the Holy Spirit. Knowing he was a hiker, I said, "The next time you are on a hike or a mountain, just begin to praise the Lord, and it will happen." And it did. Jason is a man of prayer, and he has led his flock to do likewise.

Pastor Blake Mattocks became an associate pastor at Faith Bible in Arvada and is known as Mr. YWAM for his teaching and mentorship of many students there. He is a dear friend, and a lunch or coffee or a couple minutes in his study is always encouraging.

Chris Cobb went on to earn two master's degrees and a PhD in education from Southern Seminary. He has authored two books and is writing his third. He is now director of education and a worship leader at his church in Florida. Chris and his wife, Lori, have served many years now in full-time ministry. It is always encouraging to spend time with him when they are in Denver. He always calls to set up a time, and that is so kind of him to do so.

Bob Hunt, a Joshua Nations rep since the early days, has led several trips for Joshua nations into Cuba. He has served in the children's ministry at Faith Bible Chapel in Arvada for 15 years. We have traveled to Cuba many times, and he headed up a conference to show teachers how to use a children's curriculum developed for Joshua Nations. He is a loyal and faithful friend to me. His life is a great testimony to others.

Steve Owings planted and pastored Living Waters church in Lafayette, Colorado. He also travels with Global Awakening and ministers faith, healing, and deliverance in many nations in Asia. He and his wife, Christi (a published author), have pastored for more than a dozen years in Frederick and Lafayette, Colorado. He is a Joshua Nations Rep, and we have taken numerous trips together in nations such as Myanmar and Thailand and in Africa.

Steve and Christi are true servants. As I travel with them, they exude with serving their team members and are very gracious and generous. We traveled a recent trip to Sierra Leone when we became fast friends with our Moslem driver. We plied him with candy, food, and other goodies. In one of our meetings he accepted Jesus and couldn't wait for the trip to be over, so he could tell his family about Jesus. What joy for all of us when Steve baptized him in the hotel swimming pool!

Scott Smith established the YWAM base in Homer, Alaska, and has directed that great work for over 20 years influencing hundreds of lives. While at RMBI the students had to put together a ministry plan for what they would do after they graduated. Scott's plan was to start a YWAM base in Alaska, and that's what he did.

Heather Bilyou has been working with and ministering to children at the Faith Bible Chapel day care. She has been on several missions trips to Cuba and King Jesus, North Pole, Alaska. She has a faithful spirit and loves Jesus.

One of our faithful grads is **Brian Semmen,** who was so instrumental in publishing our monthly newsletter for Joshua Nations for the first six years. He and his wife, Marla, serve in their church in Aurora, Colorado.

After graduating, **Steve Maestos** went on to plant and pastor a church in Littleton.

At that time there several students who attended Victory Outreach Center in Denver. One was **Cesar Portillo,** who after graduation went to South Africa and planted many churches, was a great evangelist, and now serves in his church as their Bible School director and speaks all over the country. He is an exceptional leader and sets the bar high!

Another Victory Outreach student was **Marisol** who serves full time in her church in administration.

Pastor Mateo also served many years in Victory Outreach and planted a congregation in Chicago.

Joe DeMott, Jr. planted a church called Refiner's Fire in Thornton, Colorado.

He and his wife, Rebecca, are committed to helping others find God's call on their lives, then train and release them into that call.

One of my greatest joys is for a former student to work full time with us. **Jack Gaudin,** while at RMBI, found his call to be a chaplain with the Good News Jail and Prison Ministry in Cañon City. He served for 10 years in the 23-hour lock-down prison and ministered to the worst of the worst from the world's standpoint, including death row inmates. The Lord used Jack in miraculous ways, leading hundreds to Christ, delivering them from demonic spirits, and discipling them to walk in freedom.

During that time, the Holy Spirit infused in him the same passion He'd been giving me: a heart for reaching the nations. One of those trips was my third trip to Pakistan in 2007. Jack then came to serve as a Joshua Nations rep in 2010 and traveled to 28 nations in training leaders to start Bible Training Centers, teaching in pastor's conferences, and teaching church planting.

Brad Matherne graduated and served as an associate pastor alongside his father at Praise Church in Littleton. He is now the senior pastor of the church and is prospering in the ministry there.

Kelly Morrison, daughter of Pastor George Morrison, served on staff at Faith Bible Chapel with the women's and Israel ministry. She is married to Rod Ginn, and together they serve in their church in Atlanta, Georgia.

Another graduate, **Ruben Magana,** served on staff for Faith Bible Chapel for 15 years. The Lord gave him a vision to start a ministry to the homeless to give them a hand up, Champions for Him. He earned his bachelor's degree at Colorado Christian University.

Erick Olsen came to us with a degree from the Colorado School of Mines in Golden. He earned a master's degree in social work and was a youth pastor in Scotland for eight years. He is now a counselor in the Denver public school system.

Don Bruce graduated from RMBI and became administrative dean for me, a tremendous asset to me and RMBI. He served in that capacity until the school closed. Recently he and his wife, Myrna, lost everything they had to the floods in Florida. It was a devastating blow, but Don and Myrna had incredible attitudes during the relocation process. They are my heroes.

Jim Dennis worked for several nonprofits and is now retired but is the prayer coordinator for Joshua Nations. Very, very important!

Brandy Graham returned to South Carolina, married to Ryan, has four children, and has taken mission trips and serves in her home church there. She has been a great encouragement to our lives.

Chris Ingalls served in the Faith Bible Chapel youth department and was integral in the establishing of Novation Church. He is currently the president of the board of directors and is the director of spiritual growth.

Ryan Smith served as a youth pastor of an Assembly of God church in Washington and has been the associate pastor under Tim Lovell for 6 years in Australia.

These are a few of the RMBI graduates and how God is using them. I am so grateful for each and every one of the 500 students who graduated from RMBI during those 14 years.

More Impact Around the World through Joshua Nations

These are just a few brief stories of some of the ways the Holy Spirit moved and is moving in the nations through Joshua Nations reps and friends. There are so many other stories to tell, but this should give a tiny snapshot.

Africa

By January 2010, the Lord had established 122 BTCs in Burundi, the Congo, Rwanda, Ghana, Kenya, the Verde Islands, and Zimbabwe. In Uganda, with 87 leaders trained, we noted the potential of 15,000 students soon, adding to the existing 1,463 students that we counted.

Rwanda, Africa

September 2010, after visiting the Genocide Museum, I wrote, "The heart of the Father weeps over the cruelty of the genocide (in Rwanda, a million killed in 90 days) wars that have left crippling scars, both in the natural and spiritual realms. Jim and Pam Behler, Jack Gaudin, Greg Johnsen, and I ministered salvation, hope, healing, and deliverance to so many spiritually hungry people. Precious men, women, and children were healed and set free from incredible ... emotional wounds." God manifested His power, grace, peace, mercy, and love throughout these desperate nations.

We witnessed this in northern Uganda after the Kony rebellion.

Kenya, Africa

On one trip, we traveled across four nations—many dusty miles packed shoulder-to-shoulder in a van. Two weeks of our life's service yielded an eternal harvest of souls for hundreds of African people on that trip. More than 400 Africans professed faith in Jesus as their Lord and Savior.

Along with Jack Gaudin and others, we also distributed rice and beans, organized by a local group, which fed 720 pygmies for one week. And provided funds to undergird four new ministries. The Holy Spirit opened doors for Pastor Faith O'Halloran and Angela Thomas (an attorney from Kansas City) to train more than 40 teachers with the JN children's curriculum and distribute gifts and school supplies to 150 children.

Batwa Pygmy tribes in Burundi and the Congo

Burundi, a landlocked country in east-central Africa, is bordered by the Democratic Republic of the Congo to the west, Tanzania to the east and south, and the small war-torn country of Rwanda to the north. The Pygmies, averaging 5 feet in height, specialize in pottery, which they sell, and others hunt. We saw great poverty there, with makeshift huts of rags and sticks.

We launched schools with the Pygmy tribes in 2009.

Ghana, Africa: A Good Meal and the Last Book

Fifty leaders in Ghana gathered to learn how to start Bible Training Centers. As usual, we fed our trainees good meals, the kind they are not used to. I stood outside a screen window as they ate their dinner.

"I have never had a meal as good as this in all my life," I heard one bush pastor say. "God has blessed me because of my faithfulness."

I turned my head, weeping. My heart filled with extreme gratitude to God for allowing me to bless this precious pastor. To think he praised God for a simple meal!

We throw away in America what these hidden heroes in a jungle village consider a meal fit for a king.

Later at that training, we ran out of books and materials. At the end, an elegant lady dressed fashionably Ghanaian came up to me and asked me for a copy of the curriculum. I had only the one I taught from.

She saw it and begged me for it. What could I do? It had my notes. It had my thoughts! After I looked into her eyes at her spirit and her intense desire, I handed it to her.

She started to jump up and down, robe colors blurring, thanking me profusely with tears and exuberant joy.

Curriculum Chaos in the Congo

The last of the daylight peered through the blown-out windows from war in this congregation as I spoke to 40 African bishops. I explained how the next day in training would go.

They expected 50 leaders, but 90 or more showed up, their beautiful black faces intense with a hunger to learn how to study and set up a Bible Training Center. They held up books, showed truths to each other, excitedly clutching the materials.

When the time came to pass out the books, chaos broke loose. One of the bishops tottered forward, loaded down with the limited supply of books to pass out. I heard a noise that grew louder and louder and saw a crowd of ladies belting out their African chant.

They rushed toward the man of God, shoving, pushing—grabbing at the books—and almost knocked the good ole boy down.

Thailand: God Moves on Elephant Mountain

In early 2013, I traveled with Lana to Thailand, where we conducted a "Mighty Move of God" conference with Dr. Aje and Nancy and the Akha Foundation. Pastors Dave and Dee Dee Thompson (of Gateway to Mount Zion church in Golden, Colorado) taught with me and ministered strong spiritual breakthroughs with the Akha leaders.

One of the highlights of the services took place on Elephant Mountain. Moved by the Holy Spirit, the men of the village got down on their knees and repented for the way they've treated their women over the years. Rarely does this happen with American men, never mind Akha men who grow up in a culture where they rule over women. In a service that lasted five long hours, men wept with broken hearts and laughed for joy for the forgiveness and freedom Christ showered on them.

About five years earlier, Stan Jacobson, Aje, a couple of the village kids, and I rode ("bounced!") up Elephant Mountain in a battered van to Dr. Aje's home. As we crested the top of the mountain, a man ran out of his hut and pounded on Aje's window.

Aje rolled it down and the man told him, "I and my family want to become Christians!"

We piled out of the van and crowded inside his dark little hut.

Aje led his entire family to Christ, then scooped up false god statues they kept and put them in a sack, which we carted off later and tossed down the mountain.

"Okay, now build a church!" Stan and I told him.

When we conducted the "Mighty Move of God" conference, it thrilled me to learn that not only does he pastor that church he started, but 20 families have come to know Jesus. Lana and I agreed, *This is why we go!*

We also got to participate in our first Akha Joshua Nations graduation. One of the young ladies traveled to a place with very few Christians, planted 20 churches, and has led more than a thousand people to Christ.

What an honor to partner with Aje and Nancy in the Lord's harvest. We left Thailand with a greater urgency to blanket the earth with the good news and Bible Training Centers.

Cuba

I've been taking teams into Cuba since 2001, when Sam Santos invited us to come. We go every year in January and sometimes also at other times of the year, and at the time of this writing, for 17 years. We've had the privilege of seeing the Holy Spirit work miracles and open the most unheard of, amazing doors on the island.

In 2003, Russ Tatro offered his Spanish curriculum seven miles in the air. After our third trip in January 2004, I realized we really needed that curriculum—Sam wept on the phone when I told him I had it. After we found a printing press in Cuba that would print it for 67 cents a book (67 cents for a years' worth of material), we started using it in 2005.

In January 2006, we took our largest group ever, 23 people—logistically very difficult (we'll never do that again!)—forming smaller groups and ministering in churches, many just an alleyway with a tarp over it. This was before Joshua Nations was officially formed, but God was putting things into place to start JN Bible Training Centers.

Often, we've teamed up with Global Advance—they'd bring in Frontline Shepherd's conferences on the front end and Joshua Nations would train leaders to start Bible Training Centers on the back end. In 2010, I helped with two of those conferences in Cuba, then the JN team followed with eight graduations, graduating 1,007 students and equipping 550 leaders. At that time, the total to date was 511 schools, 14,450 students, and 4,000 graduates. The BTCs were operating in 8 major prisons, and 24 prisoners graduated. Prison guards also studied the curriculum.

I wrote in the February 2010 newsletter, "Many students are becoming pastors, teachers, counselors, church planters, evangelists, missionaries, increasing the labor force in [many] churches they represent. The Bible schools do a great job of teaching fundamentals, but we sense the need for additional advanced training after the students graduate." Always *more*… I looked to the Holy Spirit for His never-ending *more* …

One of the most exciting developments during this time in Cuba were the schools now operating in eight major prisons on the island. Twenty-four prisoners graduated. Although they couldn't attend graduation, one of prisoner's wives received their diplomas to mail to the prison graduates. Mothers also received diplomas for their sons who graduated. I'll never forget the look of one mother who stood before me, her eyes moist and a million thanks written all over her face, a look I'd never seen in 40 years of ministry.

Then we learned that 14 government officials (guards) studied the Joshua Nations curriculum!

Children's Curriculum in Cuba and Beyond

Bob Hunt led a ministry team (Mary Jane and Josh Spencer, Lisa Levesque, Sherry Johnsen, and Katrina Mausbach) that conducted a three-day conference to teach the newly developed JN children's curriculum in Santa Clara and Havana. Comments from some of the nearly 300 attendees included "We have never seen anything like this before in Cuba. Please come back soon."

Officials from the Assemblies of God organization expressed how they appreciated the spirit of excellence in the teaching and materials and said they'd like to use it to teach their children in their 3,000-plus churches. Only the Lord knows how many children will come to know Him and learn His ways through the JN children's curriculum.

Yolanda McKenzie (who has worked with us in Mexico and her home country, Guatamala, with her husband, Jim) translated the children's curriculum into Spanish.

Bob Hunt and his team trained teachers how to teach the children's curriculum.

Latest Cuba Stats from the Leaders There

I recently returned from taking a team of 14 (January 2018) coordinated by our very capable and dedicated Bob Hunt. Some of the visas didn't come through until we were already on our way—a bit nerve-wracking, but God took care of us.

I asked for reports from the leaders in Cuba, and their news greatly encouraged me! See below.

Cuba Statistics

From the leadership in Cuba
Stats as of February 2018

It all started in Cuba! Before I met Russ Tatro and he gave us the curriculum. Before Joshua Nations was born. So the thread that runs through the growth for Joshua Nations runs thick through Cuba.

- 2001 - Started going into Cuba
- 2005 - Started Curriculum in Cuba

  SUMMARY in 2018:

- Now approaching 76,000 students trained in the BTCs
- Printed over 150,000 sets of curriculum
- Printed 15,000 Holy Spirit manuals
- Being tracked by 17 coordinators in Cuba
- 95% of the 18,320 grads are in full-time ministry (Usually 35% is good) - as apostles, prophets, pastors, teachers, evangelists

- Cubans starting schools and planting churches in 11 nations
- The churches are packed!
- Multitudes are coming to the Lord all over the island in 30 denominations.
- Leading to 2 million believers on the island
- The Assemblies of God have 80,000–100,000 leaders that we will train in these days ahead.
- There are more than 3,000 AG BTCs in Cuba.

According to the sources on the island, no other organization and discipleship training program has had the impact that Joshua Nations has had in Cuba.

We are setting up pastors' conferences to further strengthen the churches, pastors, and leaders in Cuba. Therefore we will print thousands more books and are increasing our intensity on the island as it approaches a government shift. As of this writing we don't know what that means.

But, praise God, the numbers don't tell the whole glorious story!

About the Author

Russ and Lana Frase have been married and in ministry since 1968. Dr. Frase received his bachelor's degree from Purdue University, a master of divinity degree from Southwestern Baptist Theological Seminary, and a doctor of ministry degree from Luther Rice Seminary. Since 1968, Dr. Frase has ministered in 68 nations.

Together Russ and Lana have planted churches and pastored churches for 24 years. Dr. Frase created and accredited Rocky Mountain Bible Institute in Arvada, Colorado, where he served as dean for 14 years. As a highly sought after speaker, teacher, and pastor, he has conducted revival meetings and seminars across the United States. Russ and Lana have been hosts for TBN and Daystar television programs. Additionally, Dr. Frase has served as an elder at Faith Bible Chapel for more than 30 years.

In the last 12 years as President and Founder of Joshua Nations, he has directed the establishing of 7,300 Bible Training Centers in 60 nations, in 56 languages, with more than 153,000 students and 35,000 graduates, who are in a multitude of ministry positions all over the world. Dr. Frase, with others, conducts leadership seminars with a focus on teaching, equipping, and empowering a large labor force for the body of Christ.

He has written a manual, *The Holy Spirit: The Person, Work and Ministry of the Holy Spirit*, which has been translated into 12 languages. The manual is being used in Bible study groups, youth groups, prisons, and churches in many states.

Russ and Lana reside in Westminster, Colorado, near their grown children, Paula and Rusty, and three spectacular grandsons.

Acknowledgments

There have been so many people over the past 50 years who have made me who and what I am. Only heaven knows their tremendous input and counsel in my life. The one who keeps all records knows so well and has and will reward them.

Russ Frase, Jr.
Former Dean of Rocky Mountain Bible Institute and
Founder of Joshua Nations in 2007

As with any major undertaking, producing *Runways of the Heart* has been a team effort and would not have been birthed in this form without the prayers, skills, support, sacrifices, and encouragement of many people who insisted that Pastor Russ's journey with the Holy Spirit be captured in a book. Though it took more than four years to complete, God's timing is perfect. Turns out, as you know, the Holy Spirit orchestrated it so we'd launch the book during the 50th anniversary year of Pastor Russ's service in ministry. A special blessing.

I am grateful for the Holy Spirit's transforming power in my own life while working on this project. When God calls us to a work, He's more interested in how we grow as we journey on that path. In ways that I can't express, the runways of my own heart expanded through lessons and personal growth in the many shifting and unexpected winds of the Holy Spirit.

I am deeply grateful to Pastor Russ, who had the foresight and faith in me to ask me to collaborate with him. We both had to press in when the enemy and obstacles tried to thwart us from the mission at various times and in various ways. Pastor Russ has taught me so much about what it means to walk as a person of integrity and godly character—yet with humor and unashamed humanness. There were times when I was struggling with a personal issue, and I'd be transcribing an interview with him where he had shared truths, and God would give me a *rhema* word for my situation through that!

Tremendous appreciation goes to my very understanding husband, Chet Benroth, who patiently put up with me, prayed for me, and stood by me in every way. He sacrificially overlooked more clutter and confusion in the home during heavy project deadlines and took up the slack. A faithful supporter of Pastor Russ and Joshua Nations, he always held to the belief that this story would impact the Body of Christ in life-changing ways.

Thanks also go to two very special friends, Vicki Bustos and Cathy Smiley, who came alongside and helped in ways too numerous to mention. They both love Pastor Russ and Lana very much, and they supported me through the years with their unwavering prayers and practical feedback on the book as Advance Readers. The book and Pastor Russ's travels were often subjects of prayer by the monthly Upper Room group Cathy leads.

When we finally got a draft ready around March 2018, several other people agreed to step up to the plate and be Advance Readers, offering valuable feedback from a readers' perspective that enriched the book and helped us know what details to change or add to. Special thanks to Arlene Baker, Rebecca Bishopriggs, Deanie Bodette, Dave Carlson, Kerri Lockwood Doody, Julie Entringer, Lanette Glover, Dale Jensen, Tanja Lindstrom King, Cathy McIntosh, Sheila Patrick, Lani Rogers, Peter Taylor, and Lorel Zander.

Adding to this long list of people who participated in some way to help on this book are the many Joshua Nations reps and friends of Pastor Russ's who took the time to tell their stories. Even those that did not make it into the book helped to round out information that we needed to give a more complete picture.

The Holy Spirit opened so many unexpected doors during my research that made things fun! An unexpected surprise and blessing: Denver International Airport (DIA) Air Traffic Controller Mike Anderson (a friend of Carl and Lani Rogers) gained security clearance at DIA and gave us a fascinating tour. It is the second largest airport in the world at 53 square miles. Mike graciously took Pastor Russ, Lana, Vicki, and me through the TRACON center where he works and the DIA Control Tower. We learned a lot more about the behind-the-scenes activity on the six busy runways and airspace at DIA.

I'm grateful for the tour that Anthony, a student at Denver's Metro State University, gave Pastor Russ, Lana, and me of that hidden gem, The World Indoor Airport, with 13 flight simulators. We got to see flight plans in action on the simulators. And for the insights of one who often plows snow from DIA runways as equipment operator, Matt Glover.

And my dad's best friend since first grade, Jack Blosser (a super sharp 90-year-old), gave invaluable insights to me. As a former commercial pilot and flight simulator instructor, Jack gave me technical airplane terminology and information that didn't make it into the book, but nonetheless provided backdrop for the story.

Special thanks to our production team: Melinda of Martin Publishing Services for her professional cover design and internal formatting the book; editor Marjorie Vawter, who ensured consistency with professional publishing standards; and proofreader Libby Gontarz, who provided painstaking care for accuracy and nit-picking details. Also a big thank you to Joshua Nations board member Matt Coffman, who is a never-ending support and created the illustrations above the chapter titles.

And thanks to many others—you know who you are!

And finally, all glory goes to God for the great things He has done through His Holy Spirit! He orchestrates divine appointments and circumstances in individual lives and all around the world and opens doors that no man can shut. His love is vast. Great is His faithfulness.

Marla Lindstrom Benroth
Runways of the Heart Collaborator and Project Manager
Would love your feedback, comments and stories
TellYourStoryToo@msn.com

APPENDIX A
How to Receive Christ

1. **Realize** that Jesus took your place, paying the ultimate cost by dying on the cross to purchase your salvation and you are committing your life to be His disciple.

2. **Admit** that you are a sinner, repent, and accept God's forgiveness.

    "For everyone has sinned, falling short of God's glorious standard" (Romans 3:23, NLT).

    "For all have sinned and fall short of the glory of God" (Romans 3:23, NIV).

    Repentance is to change one's mind, one's lifestyle, and to turn from oneself to Christ.

3. **Believe** in Jesus as your only hope of salvation.

    "And there is salvation in no one else, for there is no other name under heaven that has been given among men by which we must be saved" (Acts 4:12, NLT).

    "For God so loved the world that He gave His only begotten Son, that whoever believes in Him shall not perish but have everlasting life" (John 3:16, NKJV).

4. **Believe** in your heart and **Confess** with your mouth.

    "If you openly declare that Jesus is Lord and believe in your heart that God raised him from the dead, you will be saved. For it is by believing in your heart that you are made right with God, and it is by openly declaring your faith that you are saved" (Romans 10:9–10, NLT).

Salvation Prayer

Lord Jesus, I believe that You died on the cross for my sins, and I repent and turn from my sins and commit my life to be Your disciple. Forgive me, and I believe that through the shed blood of Jesus I am saved through Christ and Christ alone. I believe that You are the Son of God, raised from the dead. I believe in my heart and confess with my mouth that You, Jesus, are Lord.

APPENDIX B
How to Receive the Baptism in the Holy Spirit

1. **Be born again.**

    "The natural man does not receive the things of the Spirit" (1 Corinthians 2:14).

2. **Believe it is a biblical experience.**

    Joel 2:28–32; Luke 3:16; Acts 2

3. **Be Thirsty for the Holy Spirit.**

    "On the last day, that great day of the feast, Jesus stood and cried out, saying, 'If anyone is thirsty, let him come to Me and drink. He who believes in Me as the Scripture has said, out of his heart will flow rivers of living water.' But this He spoke concerning the Spirit, whom those believing in Him would receive; for the Holy Spirit was not yet given, because Jesus was not yet glorified" (John 7:37–39).

4. **Believe Jesus is the baptizer in the Holy Spirit.**

    "I indeed baptize you with water; but . . . He will baptize you with the Holy Spirit and fire" (Luke 3:16).

5. **Pray in faith with expectation that you will get what you ask for.**

    "If you then, being evil, know how to give gifts to your children, how much more will your Father who is in heaven give good things to those who ask Him!" (Matthew 7:11).

6. **Surrender completely to the Holy Spirit.**

Holy Spirit Baptism Prayer

Lord Jesus, I know the baptism in the Holy Spirit is a Bible truth, and I am thirsty, and I come to You who loves to baptize in the Holy Spirit. I now ask You to baptize me, to fill me with the Holy Spirit, and I know You will give me what I ask for.

It is my personal belief that one can and should speak in the spiritual gift of tongues when they receive the baptism in the Holy Spirit. In the book of Acts, the normative evidence was the gift of tongues.

That being said, there are multitudes of great leaders and Christians who have been baptized and filled with the Holy Spirit who did not exemplify the gift of tongues, yet they shook the world. Each has to move within the spiritual context they choose and desire. There is much to say about those who have gifts of the Spirit, who are most spiritual, who are in no way less than those who speak in tongues.

APPENDIX C
Key Scriptures

Referenced from www.Biblegateway.com
in the New King James Version

John 16:13-15

13 However, when He, the Spirit of truth, has come, He will guide you into all truth; for He will not speak on His own authority, but whatever He hears He will speak; and He will tell you things to come. 14 He will glorify Me, for He will take of what is Mine and declare it to you. 15 All things that the Father has are Mine. Therefore I said that He [a]will take of Mine and declare it to you.

Acts 2:1-15
Coming of the Holy Spirit

2 When the Day of Pentecost had fully come, they were all with one accord in one place. 2 And suddenly there came a sound from heaven, as of a rushing mighty wind, and it filled the whole house where they were sitting. 3 Then there appeared to them] divided tongues, as of fire, and *one* sat upon each of them. 4 And they were all filled with the Holy Spirit and began to speak with other tongues, as the Spirit gave them utterance.

The Crowd's Response

5 And there were dwelling in Jerusalem Jews, devout men, from every nation under heaven. 6 And when this sound occurred, the multitude came together, and were confused, because everyone heard them speak in his own language. 7 Then they were all amazed and marveled, saying to one another, "Look, are not all these who speak Galileans? 8 And how *is it that* we hear, each in our own language in which we were born? 9 Parthians and Medes and Elamites, those dwelling in Mesopotamia, Judea and Cappadocia,

Pontus and Asia, [10] Phrygia and Pamphylia, Egypt and the parts of Libya adjoining Cyrene, visitors from Rome, both Jews and proselytes, [11] Cretans and Arabs—we hear them speaking in our own tongues the wonderful works of God." [12] So they were all amazed and perplexed, saying to one another, "Whatever could this mean?"

[13] Others mocking said, "They are full of new wine."

Peter's Sermon

[14] But Peter, standing up with the eleven, raised his voice and said to them, "Men of Judea and all who dwell in Jerusalem, let this be known to you, and heed my words. [15] For these are not drunk, as you suppose, since it is *only* the third hour of the day."

1 Corinthians 12
Spiritual Gifts: Unity in Diversity

12 Now concerning spiritual *gifts*, brethren, I do not want you to be ignorant: [2] You know that you were Gentiles, carried away to these dumb[l] idols, however you were led. [3] Therefore I make known to you that no one speaking by the Spirit of God calls Jesus accursed, and no one can say that Jesus is Lord except by the Holy Spirit.

[4] There are diversities of gifts, but the same Spirit. [5] There are differences of ministries, but the same Lord. [6] And there are diversities of activities, but it is the same God who works all in all. [7] But the manifestation of the Spirit is given to each one for the profit *of all*: [8] for to one is given the word of wisdom through the Spirit, to another the word of knowledge through the same Spirit, [9] to another faith by the same Spirit, to another gifts of healings by the same Spirit, [10] to another the working of miracles, to another prophecy, to another discerning of spirits, to another *different* kinds of tongues, to another the interpretation of tongues. [11] But one and the same Spirit works all these things, distributing to each one individually as He wills.

Unity and Diversity in One Body

[12] For as the body is one and has many members, but all the members of that one body, being many, are one body, so also *is* Christ. [13] For by one Spirit we were all baptized into one body—whether Jews or Greeks, whether slaves or free—and have all been made to drink [into one Spirit. [14] For in fact the body is not one member but many.

[15] If the foot should say, "Because I am not a hand, I am not of the body," is it therefore not of the body? [16] And if the ear should say, "Because I am not an eye, I am not of the body," is it therefore not of the body? [17] If the whole body *were* an eye, where *would be* the hearing? If the whole *were* hearing, where *would be* the smelling? [18] But now God has set the members, each one of them, in the body just as He pleased. [19] And if they were all one member, where *would* the body *be?*

[20] But now indeed *there are* many members, yet one body. [21] And the eye cannot say to the hand, "I have no need of you"; nor again the head to the feet, "I have no need of you." [22] No, much rather, those members of the body which seem to be weaker are necessary. [23] And those *members* of the body which we think to be less honorable, on these we bestow greater honor; and our unpresentable *parts* have greater modesty, [24] but our presentable *parts* have no need. But God composed the body, having given greater honor to that *part* which lacks it, [25] that there should be no schism in the body, but *that* the members should have the same care for one another. [26] And if one member suffers, all the members suffer with *it;* or if one member is honored, all the members rejoice with *it.*

[27] Now you are the body of Christ, and members individually. [28] And God has appointed these in the church: first apostles, second prophets, third teachers, after that miracles, then gifts of healings, helps, administrations, varieties of tongues. [29] *Are* all apostles? *Are* all prophets? *Are* all teachers? *Are* all workers of miracles? [30] Do all have gifts of healings? Do all speak with tongues? Do all interpret? [31] But earnestly desire the best gifts. And yet I show you a more excellent way.

Romans 12:3-8
Serve God with Spiritual Gifts

[3] For I say, through the grace given to me, to everyone who is among you, not to think *of himself* more highly than he ought to think, but to think soberly, as God has dealt to each one a measure of faith. [4] For as we have many members in one body, but all the members do not have the same function, [5] so we, *being* many, are one body in Christ, and individually members of one another. [6] Having then gifts differing according to the grace that is given to us, *let us use them:* if prophecy, *let us prophesy* in proportion to our faith; [7] or ministry, *let us use it* in *our* ministering; he who teaches, in teaching; [8] he who exhorts, in exhortation; he who gives, with liberality; he who leads, with diligence; he who shows mercy, with cheerfulness.

Ephesians 4:7-16
Spiritual Gifts

[7] But to each one of us grace was given according to the measure of Christ's gift. [8] Therefore He says:
"When He ascended on high,
He led captivity captive,
And gave gifts to men."
[9] (Now this, "He ascended"—what does it mean but that He also first descended into the lower parts of the earth? [10] He who descended is also the One who ascended far above all the heavens, that He might fill all things.)

[11] And He Himself gave some *to be* apostles, some prophets, some evangelists, and some pastors and teachers, [12] for the equipping of the saints for the work of ministry, for the edifying of the body of Christ, [13] till we all come to the unity of the faith and of the knowledge of the Son of God, to a perfect man, to the measure of the stature of the fullness of Christ; [14] that we should no longer be children, tossed to and fro and carried about with every wind of doctrine, by the trickery of men, in the cunning craftiness of deceitful plotting, [15] but, speaking the truth in love, may grow up in all things into Him who is the head—Christ— [16] from whom the whole body, joined and knit together by what every joint supplies, according to the effective working by which every part does its share, causes growth of the body for the edifying of itself in love.

I Peter 4:10

As each one has received a gift, minister it to one another, as good stewards of the manifold grace of God.

The Gifts of the Holy Spirit in Demonstration

Gifts of Revelation

Word of Wisdom	A divine portion of wisdom imparted by the Holy Spirit as He wills to know what to do or say or be in any given situation. It is given to a person to know how to apply truth, knowledge, or information at the right time in the right way. It increases as one studies, prays, and meditates in the Psalms, Proverbs, Job, and Ecclesiastes.
Word of Knowledge John 4:47–50 Woman at the well	Information that cannot be known in any other way than by the Holy Spirit, i.e., what a person's name is without prior knowledge. This gift can open doors to an answer, healing, salvation, or a wonder-work of God in that person's life
Discerning of Spirits Acts 16 Apostle Paul and the woman with the gift of divination	The grace of God to see into the unseen realm of the spirit world to know what is really going on in any given situation. It is the spiritual impartation to discern, judge, or distinguish between the spirit of Satan and the Holy Spirit. It gives us the ability to know the difference between the false or counterfeit and the truth or real. We can judge whether a message or matter is of God or not.

Gifts of Inspiration

Prophecy 1 Corinthians 14:1, 39	Edifies or builds up the believer and spiritually advances by strengthening and encouraging. It exhorts or stirs a believer up and spurs him on with a challenge by the truth being spoken. It also comforts. According to Paul, everyone should desire and covet this gift.
Tongues Three manifestations	*Pentecost* (Acts 2): In known languages that required no interpretation. When the fire appeared on the heads of the disciples in the upper room, they spoke the good works of God in languages the speakers had never learned. *Private* (1 Corinthians 12:10): They are a powerful private prayer language, or special spiritual language encouraged by Paul for all believers. Only the Holy Spirit knows what is being spoken, and He will interpret these sacred secrets to the speaker as He wills. The Holy Spirit prays through the person the perfect will of God. *Public* (1 Corinthians 12:28, 30): The gift of tongues spoken in a public service where an interpretation is required. When Paul said, "Do all speak in tongues?" he was referring to the fact that not everyone will manifest the gift of tongues in public worship.
Interpretation of Tongues 1 Corinthians 12:10	The ability given by the Holy Spirit to interpret a message given in tongues. Since the spiritual gift of tongues is not know by the speaker or the hearer, there must be an interpretation. When a message in tongues comes forth in public worship, those who have the gift of tongues should begin to pray immediately for the Holy Spirit to interpret the message. This also can be used in one's private life. When you begin to pray in tongues, the perfect way to pray, ask the Holy Spirit to give you the interpretation. Many times He will.

Gifts of Power

Faith	Faith allows one to accomplish mighty works, turning vision into a finished product. It is the Holy Spirit empowering one to take steps of faith to do what seems naturally impossible. It is a *special* gift of faith given in the face of incredible odds, a *separate* faith given for a certain work and a faith that is not already inside man but released by the Holy Spirit inside him. Examples: Daniel in the lion's den and David and Goliath.
Working of Miracles	Supernatural intervention that interrupts, suspends, halts, or terminates the natural order. The word *miracles* indicates explosions of the almightiness of God or an astonishing work of God that usually comes instantly and is outside the range of human ability.
Gift(s) of Healing Spirit: Isaiah 53:5 Soul: Luke 4:18 Body: Gospels and Acts	*Gifts* is plural because there are different gifts given to people in certain areas of sicknesses. It is the supernatural power given by the Holy Spirit to heal the spirit, soul (mind, will, and emotions), and physical body of a person. These gifts have the ability to heal all manner of diseases, ailments, infirmities, and pain without the aid of natural means.

—Excerpted from the training manual, *The Holy Spirit: The Person, Work and Ministry of the Holy Spirit*, by Dr. Russ Frase, Jr. Copyright 2015.

Runways of the Heart: My Journey Empowered by the Holy Spirit and *The Holy Spirit* training manual available in paperback, Kindle and ePub on Amazon and where books are sold.

For more information,
go to www.JoshuaNations.org.